Life After

40

A Semi-autobiographical Guide

Fulton Books, Inc.
Meadville, PA

Published by Fulton Books 2021

ISBN 978-1-64654-224-6 (paperback)
ISBN 978-1-63860-223-1 (hardcover)
ISBN 978-1-64654-225-3 (digital)

Printed in the United States of America

Dedication

THIS BOOK IS dedicated to those that are still living the struggle with addiction, my youngest of my two sons, Austin, who never went back on his word, my older brother, Jeff, who foolishly answered that phone call the day I started my unconventional rehab, my best friend, Bryan, who bore the task of listening to every foolish thing I have ever said, and most importantly, my heart, my breath, my wife, Erin (Pickles), who stood by me while I fell to pieces.

Prologue

DO YOU KNOW how they say your life flashes before your eyes before you die?

Well... I hate to be the bearer of bad news. It doesn't, or at least, it didn't for me. Instead, it was just a bunch of people gathered around what they now call the "scene of the accident" with their cell phones out trying to capture the last moments of my life on video so they can get their next fifteen minutes of Facebook fame that's measured by shocked face and thumbs-up emojis while you're looking up at an unfamiliar face that's screaming at the top of their lungs "Clear!" just before shocking you with enough electricity to power a small country.

There was no bright light at the end of a tunnel, but instead, several red-and-blue flashing ones that were on top of the squad car that the friendly officer, who was trying to figure out precisely what had happened, arrived in and a bright street light I was lying under, laughing out loud at my current situation while repeating over and over, "Well played, karma, well played."

It would take another shock and some injections before I heard the unfamiliar face that was trying to save my life tell the friendly officer who was now questioning a man that seemed to forget how to button and zip his pants about what had happened. "He's stable, but we have to move him now," leaving me to believe that the unfamiliar face had no clue what he was talking about because, at that point in my life, I was anything but stable.

Now, as much as I would like to tell you what left me in the street that night was some kind of a heroic effort on my part, that would be the furthest from the truth. In fact, I bet if you asked around, most people would tell you I deserved to be there that night, and I can't say I disagree. No, this isn't one of those hero stories; in fact, it's a whole lot less complicated than that.

It's just a poorly written story about life, love, addiction, along with some other stuff.

Chapter 1

And So, It Begins

THERE ARE A million different ways I could start this semi-autobiographical story about life, love, addiction, along with some other stuff from the classic "It was the best of times, it was the worst of times" to the most commonly used "You wouldn't believe me if I told you," but I think it would be best to simply start from the beginning. It all started on September 2, 2013. An easy enough date to remember because it was precisely seven days since I moved back into the home I shared with my wife of twenty-some-odd years, Marie, twenty-eight days since I ended a three-year relationship with pain pills, and exactly forty years since I came into this world. That's right; it's my birthday and not just any birthday, but my fortieth, making me officially over the hill.

The day started just like any other. I woke up to the guy on the radio telling me, "It's going to be a beautiful day," as I stumbled into the bathroom for a shower and a quick shave before heading to the kitchen to meet Marie at the coffeepot for our daily meeting that consisted of what bills needed to be paid or which, with a decent enough excuse, could go until next payday without something being shut off due to lack of payment. After the meeting was adjourned, Marie kissed me softly on the cheek just before whispering in my ear, "I still love you, sexy man," which I found hard to believe. Not that she was lying, except for the sexy part, because after twenty-some-odd years of being married, I'm pretty sure the sexy part she mentioned was gone if it ever existed at all, but the "I love you." I mean, how could she? After all, I had just put her through, but for some reason, she did.

I first met Marie the summer before my senior year of high school around the time "text messages" were still called "notes," MTV still played music videos, and radio airplay was being taken over by a band who had a number one song about a brand of deodorant. I was supposed to be working the grave-yard shift at my stepdad's new business but instead was standing outside waiting on a delivery of what we called "Mary-Jane" from my local florist and best friend Lennie that I would then share with some of my stepdad's other employees...for a small fee, of course.

I met Lennie at one of several burger places I worked at before landing the cushy job at my stepdad's company, and even though he had graduated a couple of years before me from the same high school where I was still in the hopeful stages of my academic career, we hit it off and have been best friends ever since.

At around six feet tall with blond curly hair, Lennie looked a lot older than his actual age of nineteen, which was a plus when it came to someone asking him for an ID while he was buying beer before we would cruise up and down the strip located in front of the local shopping mall on the few and far in-between days his car wasn't parked safely at the mechanic's place where it refused to move.

When Lennie finally showed up that night the same way he usually showed up anywhere—in a borrowed car and late. I was more than a little surprised to see Marie sitting in the rear passenger side seat of the car Lennie borrowed from her. She had shoulder-length strawberry-blond hair, crystal-blue eyes with just a hint of trouble behind them, and a smile that lit up the loading dock, I was standing on that night, leaving me for the first time in my seventeen years speechless.

We were far from a match made in heaven. After all, I was just your average, socially awkward and romantically challenged underachiever from a small town that you probably never heard of, with a face only a mother could love, whose only aspersions, at that time, were paying Lennie for his delivery without getting caught by my stepdad, starting the coolest skateboard company ever, and hopefully one day—being on the silver screen in movie credits as "Guy Eating Taco." And Marie beautiful beyond my reach, with a lot more than just a few aspirations for her future, not to mention the small town she was from had her last name on most of the buildings making her what most might call un-obtainable for a guy like me.

I don't know where I got the nerve to even introduce myself to her, even though it was just the simple nineties. "What's up?" head nod while handing Lennie a bunch of crumpled ones and fives to pay for the much-anticipated delivery. It may have been because I noticed what looked like my stepdad's brown truck pulling in to verify his suspicion that I was socializing instead of working, or aliens do exist, and I just had a close encounter of some kind, either way, I not only got her name but a date for the following Friday.

I tried to impress Marie the best way a guy with an empty bank account and in between paychecks could by packing a picnic basket with some leftover fried chicken and my mom's self-proclaimed "world-famous" potato salad that I had acquired from my parents' fridge under the "it's easier to ask for forgiveness" policy and an old blanket that I was sure no one would miss before taking her to the most romantic spot I knew called the "Falls," which was actually just a large cement drainage pipe with some graffiti on it where kids went to make out.

We spent the evening getting to know each other while dining on my recently acquired free food and as I listened to her talk about anything she wanted to, there were only two things I was sure about that night: first, *Bill & Teds*; second, adventure wasn't nearly as excellent as the original; and second, no matter where I ended up in life, I wanted Marie there with me.

Over the next several months, Marie and I became insepa-rable, spending every waking moment we could together, until about a year or so later and shortly after my parents asked me to move out of my childhood home, we decided to make our relationship official, and on March something or another 1992, in a small courthouse ceremony that consisted of only five people—me, Marie, the judge, and two witnesses, one being Lennie, of course—we became husband and wife.

Our life together started out anything but easy; some people even thought it was destined to fail maybe because of our age, my immaturity, or that Marie was pregnant with our first of two children and they felt that was the only reason we got married. Either way after twenty-some-odd years together I think it's safe to say that they didn't know what they were talking about.

After the less-than-crowded wedding, Marie and I moved into our first place together that consisted of an old blue sofa sleeper in her parents living room and I got a job at one of the local fast-food restaurants through my last few months of high school, along with being a photographer and videographer on the weekends since that cushy job at my stepdads place came to an end around the same time I was asked to move out.

I don't know where the drive came from, my love for Marie or that I was dead set on proving for the first time, according to my mom, that she was wrong when she said I wouldn't graduate high school, and even though it was only one point above passing, I graduated. Then just three short days after receiving my diploma, I traded in my cap and gown for dad shoes and adulthood.

I would work several different jobs over the next couple of years—from selling portraits in the local department stores to those hearing aids that were said to be a "Miracle" basically, anything an underachiever with barely a high school diploma like me could get a job doing until eventually, I was able to smooth-talk my way into a salesman position at the local car dealership. The hours were long and very unforgiving, but the pay was great even though it was strictly commission.

Marie worked part-time, in between being a mother to our now two sons, at the local video store to cover those months when sales weren't that good until we were finally able to save enough money to say goodbye to the sleeper sofa in her parents living room, and her dad having to yell, "Heads up!" because he was in his boxers and T-shirt, making his way to the kitchen for his double scoop of cookies-and-cream ice cream before the eleven o'clock news.

Marie and I spent several weeks and countless hours combing through ads in the local newspaper and those free "Homes for Sale" books that are at the entrance of any grocery or convenient store. Usually right next to the little red quarter machines that have cool stuff in them, like little football helmets and the always favorite "Super Ball,". Searching of for the perfect place to raise our family of four until Marie came across an ad that seemed to be written just for us that read, "Three-bedroom split-level house with a large backyard located in a quiet neighborhood, excellent schools, close to shopping."

The next day, with the scribbled down directions that Marie got from Patty, our new realtor in hand. Marie and I headed out to take a closer look at the place we would eventually call home. We spent several hours diving around our soon to be new neighborhood like tourists visiting a new country. Reading street signs, house numbers until there it was: 401 Helena Avenue. I probably would have driven right past the house if it wasn't for hearing Marie scream with excitement as she pointed at it like a kid might when you drive by the ice-cream stand, wanting you to stop for a scoop or two.

It wasn't the biggest or fanciest house in the neighborhood that one belonged to the family just down the street from us "The Joneses". And as for the close to shopping part of the ad, well, that turned out to be nothing more than a small family-owned mini-mart on the corner that carried things like milk, bread, beer, and cigarettes at state minimum prices.

After Marie composed herself from her childlike outburst, we slowly pulled into the driveway that was marked by several shrubs on one side, dividing it from the lawn and tall pine trees on the other, marking the property line while adding a little privacy from the neighbors. There was a stone walkway that made its way past a big bay window to a large, freshly painted brown door, where Patty, our realtor, was waiting with the keys. The first room you entered was the living room. It wasn't what you might call huge, but the size wasn't the main attraction; instead, it was a large stone fireplace that would be perfect for hanging Christmas stockings on for our now two sons Zachary and Austin or to snuggle in front of with Marie during our mandatory once-a-week date night that was part of our agreement when I took the job at the dealership.

To the left was the dining room where we planned to have our "How was your day?" family dinners every evening, except for Monday and Thursday because of the 9:00 a.m. until 9:00 p.m. hours that the dealership was open, making it impossible for me to join in the conversation. Connecting the dining room to the kitchen was a small bar, or "peninsula," as Patty called it, where I would serve my pan-sized pancakes every Sunday the same way my dad did for me and my brothers when we were kids. The kitchen was of average size and not very modern; instead, it looked more like something out of the 1970s, complete with matching olive green stove and refrigerator, yellow simulated marble countertops, and those orange Tupperware canisters with the push-button top that most people stored their flour, sugar, and fresh-baked cookies in. Allowing Marie to use her interior design skills that she picked up from every home and garden magazine that she read in the checkout line of the grocery store over the past couple of years.

Patty spent another hour or so showing us around the rest of the house, including the three upstairs bedrooms, the large bathroom with walk-in shower, and a spacious attic that would be perfect for storing boxes of old memories we were still in the early stages of making, but I don't think anything impressed Marie more than the small breakfast nook with the two sliding doors that lead out to a huge patio that we would later call "the watchtower," where she would sit and watch the boys play in the backyard, either on the swing set or in the sandbox that we bought for them shortly after moving in.

After Patty's grand tour of the house ended, I planned on using my recently acquired sales skills along with my gift of gab to negotiate the best price possible on the house, but those plans quickly changed under the big oak tree beside the single car garage when Marie asked, "What do you think? Babies?" with the brightest smile on her face, and that's all it took for me to say, "We'll take it." To be honest, I don't know what we even paid for it, but I was a little suspicious that we had over-paid when Patty took that weeklong Bahamas vacation she had wanted to go on for several years but never quite had the funds available until shortly after giving us the keys.

We spent the next couple of days with just the two of us moving all the secondhand furniture that we got from friends, family, and out of the local newspaper ads since our budget wouldn't allow all the fancy latest and greatest of 1995 and the unwritten rule that a friend is a friend until moving day. After everything was placed, painted, and perfect, we spent our first official date night snuggled on the floor in front of the fireplace with plans of christening our new home, but instead, it turned into Marie lying with her head in my lap fast asleep. I would have preferred to sleep in the secondhand bed I spent a couple of hours wrestling up the stairs to the second floor of the house, but I was more than happy watching her sleep right where she was.

Soon after moving in, Marie turned in her smock from the video store to be a full-time mom to our two little crumb snatchers, kissing boo-boos, making sure they brushed their teeth, along with being a full-time taxi, taking them to school in the morning, baseball in the spring and football in the fall while I spent just enough time at home because of the long hours that were required of me at work that they knew I existed.

I eventually moved through the ranks from salesman to finance manager, the hours were even more, less forgiving than before, but the pay was great keeping me neck and neck in the unspoken contest between myself and Mr. Jones from down the street, not to mention there would be no more standing on the lot in every kind of weather Mother Nature could throw at me, waiting for my next sale. Instead, the other salesman brought them to me in a large but cozy office in the back to fill out all the paperwork required to purchase any car and hopefully purchase an extended warranty, gap insurance, credit life, and disability, or as we referred to it, "choke-and-croak" for a little extra above my salary.

Life was good, Marie was happy, the boys were doing well, or at least that's what the pictures that Marie framed for my office wall that doubled as an ice breaker for the next customer I would give my sales pitch to showed. So I guess it's safe to say that at one time, I kind of had my shit together.

Now I know what you are thinking, How could someone throw everything they spent the past eighteen years or so building away, for drugs, which is an honest question, and one that I've asked myself several times before, usually after seeing one of those special news reports on the TV about the opiate epidemic we are facing today while sneaking a couple of that day-old doughnuts and a tasty cup of coffee from the service department waiting room. Well, it's a lot easier than you think. All it took was one angry customer who was paying close attention to nothing because of a service bill she didn't think she had to pay, a three-day stay in the hospital, and an abundant supply of those little demons that were said to be non-addictive, prescribed by a doctor who traded in his moral compass for large cash bonuses paid for by "Big Pharma" for writing said prescription to create the perfect storm that would, for the first time since the summer before my senior year of high school, test the strength of mine and Marie's relationship along with my sanity.

Chapter 2

And Just Like That

A LOT OF things have changed since we first got the keys to the house Marie loved so much, paying for Patty's long-awaited vacation to the Bahamas before karma first decided to make me an unwilling participant in a game I didn't want to play that would eventually lead to me lying on the street that night, looking up at the crowd that was forming, who all seemed to have the same expression on their face most people did at the end of that movie, where the kid sees dead people and you figure out his doctor was exactly where I wanted to be.

All the secondhand furniture we started out with has since been replaced with the latest trends Marie still reads about in those home-and-garden magazines. Except now instead of reading them in the checkout lane of the grocery store, she does it right from the convince of her phone—usually while waiting for me to come home after another one of those "Sorry, Pickles, I am going to be late again" calls I always seemed to be making because Mr. and Mrs. something or another wants to take their new whatever type car, truck or SUV they bought home.

The small bar, or "peninsula," as Patty called it, where I haven't made my Sunday pan-sized pancakes in quite some time, now serves as the final resting place for junk mail, expired coupons, and the coffeepot where Marie and I held our meetings at every morning before I headed out to work. The kitchen is a lot more modern than the 1970s version it was when we first looked at the house, and all the carpet has been replaced a few more times than once. Several more pictures of events I was always absent from over the years like summer vacations, holiday dinners, and high school graduations have been added to the mantle of the stone fireplace; that's the first thing you notice when you first walk through the still freshly painted brown door.

The swing set and sandbox are still in the backyard right where the boys slowly abandoned them over the years for things like skateboards, video games, and more adult stuff like cars, relationships, and lives of their own. Like I said, at one time, I had my shit together, validating, even more, my mom had no clue what she was talking about when she said that mine and Marie's relationship was nothing more than an "infatuation" and "puppy love."

Now I'm not quite sure what I did to deserve karma's undivided attention at that point in my life. It could have been because of all the little white lies I may or may not have told over the years like "it's all freeway miles" or "it's a one-owner" even though I had no clue where the car, truck, or SUV came from, let alone where it had been driven. Maybe it was because I never returned the blanket Marie and I used on our first date at the falls a little over a couple of years ago to my parents' house. Either way, I wasn't at all prepared for karma's well-planned, accidental events that started shortly after I noticed Helen Derflinger pulling on the lot in her five-month-old SUV and decided that since she was such a miserable ray of sunshine when she first begged me to get her a loan because her credit was anything but perfect that it would be best for me hide in my office and out of her line of sight.

Helen was the kind of person that the sound of her voice, or the sheer mention of her name, gives you the same feeling you get when you're ready to take a long-anticipated shower, only to find out that the person before you did not use the hot water sparingly enough for anyone else. We have all met or seen someone like Helen—usually at the counter of any fast-food restaurant, wearing every kind of name-brand knockoff in a sad attempt to show her importance to everyone. While demanding to see the manager because she felt "wronged" by a pickle on her cheeseburger after she clearly stated to no one but herself "no pickles" when she placed the order.

Feeling a little too confident that Helen wouldn't find me safely tucked away in my office, I decided to start my normal daily routine of checking paperwork, calling banks, and booking deals when I got a call for a very distraught Marie because our oldest son decided to exit through his bedroom window in the middle of the night to be with what he thought was his first true love since she was moving four hundred miles away that very day.

I spent the next several minutes or so trying to comfort Marie the best way I could, reassuring her that our son would be fine even though I was a little worried myself when I was rudely interrupted by the sound of Helen tapping her Lee Press-On Nails against the trim of my office door while looking over the top of her knockoff Gucci sunglasses, holding what looked like an unpaid service bill and the customer copy of the warranty I sold her. Clearly ready to start a battle of wits with me—a challenge I was more than happy to accept!

Helen started the one-sided battle by slamming the unpaid service bill and her copy of the warranty I sold her the first time we met down on my desk before claiming that I had lied to her about the extended warranty she bought, covering tire rotations and that she wasn't going to pay the fourteen-dollar service bill she was now holding and shaking about an inch to close to my face.

I quickly showed Helen where I had circled and highlighted the part of her warranty that clearly states it does not cover regular maintenance items, such as oil changes, belts, hoses, and of course, tire rotations, along with where she had initialed, acknowledging that she understood what was circled and that she was more than responsible for the unpaid service bill.

After game-set match to my favor, I quietly listened to Helen rant for about a minute or so longer before reaching into my pocket and taking out a twenty-dollar bill to throw at her as I explained to that there were far more important things going on in my life at that time than to listen to her argue over what was clearly written, leaving her the only move she could make—"I want to see your manager," which I was more than happy point her in his direction, which was far from my office and probably the safest place for her to be at that moment.

I waited until the sound of Helen's bedazzled flip-flops were far enough away from my office before sneaking outside to my favorite hiding spot, just behind what we called "delivery" row, for a quick smoke to calm down from the one-sided game of wits I had been in with Helen before calling home to check on Marie and possibly find out where my oldest sons new residence would be.

Now most people will tell you that karma doesn't have a sense of humor, but unfortunately, she does, and not the funny "haha" type but more of the "wait for it…" kind because no sooner did I step outside for my customary, every five-minute smoke, I heard Helen screaming to the top of her lungs, "I have never been spoken to that way and whatever happened to 'the customers always is always right,'" followed by my boss telling her, "Well, unfortunately, this is not one of those times," which took Helen's already glowing personality to a whole new level of mad.

There is an unwritten rule in the car business, and probably in all retail, that states, "When a customer is that mad, never make eye contact." A rule that I should have broken because maybe I would have noticed the vehicle that I was standing in front of belonged to Helen and could have moved out of the way, when as she said, "accidentally put the car in drive instead of reverse," pinning me against the door I had just come out of, cracking two ribs, breaking my leg, and knocking me unconscious.

The next thing I remember was waking up in the hospital, with my leg now in a cast, my ribs hurting so bad that I couldn't breathe, and Marie sitting in one of those small uncomfortable hospital room chairs, trying to be as strong as she could while the doctor explained everything she needed to know, like how to take care of the cast on my leg, ace bandage for my ribs since there isn't really anything else they can do with them, and finally, a small piece of paper with the name of the medicine I would be taking to help with the pain that you encounter after getting hit by a car scribbled in the normal illegible handwriting that doctors always seem to use.

The doctor prescribed me 120, 10-milligram pills called Percocet that had four refills available. Now I was never a big fan of pain meds; after all, I was brought up being told that "walking it off" is the best pain medicine, but I soon found out when you reach a certain age, walking it off isn't really an option. Besides, the doctor at the hospital prescribed them with the instructions written clearly on the bottle, "Take one tablet every four hours or as needed for pain," complete with a name, followed by the initials MD, so you would think it's safe, right? Wrong, it's what they don't write on the bottle that makes those jagged little pills so dangerous. Things like highly addictive, and how eventually they will cost you everything that ever mattered.

It would take a short week of recovering at home and me tripping on my only shoelace while trying to hand a thirty-day tag to the salesman so they could bolt on the car that the friendly people who just left my office bought during the dealership's annual three-day sale "extravaganza" that included cotton candy for the kids, a free six-piece toolset for dad "no purchase required," those rare "only happens once a year" deals on all new and used cars, topped off with "Do you have a job? Drive a car home today" guarantees for those with less-than-perfect credit customers before I would take the first pill that would eventually lead to me lying on the cold, damp street that night in a pool of my own blood, looking up at the unfamiliar face that misdiagnosed me as being stable.

It would take about an hour and two more customers before I started to feel the effects of the first pill, and all I can say is, "WOW!" I felt just like that guy, whose home planet blew up when he was just a baby, every time he comes in contact with our yellow sun, Super! All the pain in my leg and ribs seemed to just disappear, along with all the other aches and pains that come naturally with age. There was a spring in my step, even with the cast on my leg, that would be part of my daily attire for the next six to eight weeks.

My sales were up and paperwork perfect, that super feeling even made its way into mine and Marie's date night, where instead of just snuggling up after dinner to watch a late-night something or another TV show, we would instead spend that time together in the bedroom where it would require some Gatorade and two power bars for Marie to keep up with my newly re-discovered enthusiasm just like when we first met twenty-some-odd years ago. I was on top of the world, but just like that nice man from the other planet had a weakness, so did

I, his was a rock from his own planet, and mine, I would soon find out was an addiction.

At first, it was easy for me to achieve those recently discovered superpowers that came with the first pill; the hard part would be maintaining them. What had started out as one with my morning cup of service department coffee soon turned into another at lunch, then dinner, and just before bed so I could sleep all while trying to convince myself that I don't have a problem, after all, I hadn't exceeded the "four a day or as needed for pain" instructions that were clearly written on the bottle that the nice doctor sent home with me after my so-called accidental run-in with Helen's SUV.

It would take another eight months and the last of those once-prescribed pills gone before karma finally decided to reveal the "wait for it" punch line of her joke, and needless to say, I didn't find it at all funny. What was first prescribed to help me with the pain of a broken leg and a couple of ribs was now needed for me to merely function on a day-to-day basis without getting sick because of my body's demands for just one more.

Most people would think that with all the government regulations and programs that "DARE" people not to use drugs, it would be hard for anyone to get their hands on those pills without a prescription. Well, those people would be wrong. Finding them wasn't hard at all; paying for them, on the other hand, would prove to be a little more than challenging since what once cost me a mere twenty-dollar co-pay for 120 pills would now cost the going street price of a dollar a milligram, along with requiring me to go into those places that you hear about on those true crime shows I enjoy watching so much, that usually starts with the narrator saying something like "It would be the last place they were seen alive," to meet people with made-up names like "Dinner Bell" in a weak attempt to hide their real identity when the scariest thing I had ever done before was a crossword puzzle in ink.

I continued my relationship with those once recommended pills while hiding my addiction in plain sight from Marie and everyone else for about two more years. Two years of making excuses of where I had been, where I am going at this hour, and "what happened to my jewelry" that I had sold to keep feeding my habit, until one day, I came home to find a note on the door from Marie that said,

> The man I love is missing. Don't
> come back until you find him.
> —Marie

Along with everything little bit of just a few things I had left from working so hard all those years packed neatly into a small green backpack, confirming my suspicions that I had not been fooling Marie at all and that she was finally tired at looking at all the places in the house where stuff once was marked by indentations in the carpet where our top of the line furniture had once been before I sold it in one of those buy-sell groups on Facebook and all the clean places on the wall where our high-end TVs used to hang that are at their new home inside the local pawnshop.

No apology was going to be good enough, no compromise, no "let's talk about it," or false promises of things can only get better was going to work this time. Marie had drawn her line in the sand, and for the first time since never, courtesy of those once prescribed pills and my own doing, I was alone requiring me to make the hardest phone call I have ever had to make for help, which coincidently was the same number as my older brother.

Chapter 3

Wash, Rinse, and Rehab

AS I STOOD in the rain, looking at the house that had just become my previous residence, holding the backpack full of what little bit of anything I had left and the note of so few words but said so much Marie had left for me, I remembered an old saying my grandmother used to say: "You can tell the strength of a person by the decisions they make." Leaving those who knew me the least, like Marie's older sister Sharon, to think I was weak for calling my older brother and that I was just abandoning Marie to clean up the mess my addiction caused, but that would be the furthest from the truth.

A lot of things went into the decision to call my older brother, none of which had anything to do with abandoning Marie, but more of my inability to pay for what little bit professional help that's even available since my addiction had left me with just enough money in my wallet for nothing and those free places! well, they do background checks to make sure you didn't have any of what the legal system calls "outstanding warrants" that I may or may not have had one or two of at that time. Finally, I was just tired—tired of hanging out at emergency rooms at all hours of the night hoping to get a doctor that would buy my "it hurts enough" for them to write me a prescription or spending what little money I had with one of the many connects I had made over the years, all while trying to hide my addiction in plain sight from Marie.

At just six days short of a year older and a few inches taller than me, my older brother has that Southern boy charm with matching accent, an "I'll try anything once" attitude, who's not afraid to tell you precisely what you don't want to hear, and knows just enough about everything to make him what some may call "overly confident" basically everything I needed to finally get clean.

Now, as strange as this sounds, coming from a guy that had just lost everything in a matter of minutes, but as we pulled into the driveway of my brother's bachelor mansion that was surrounded by several "I'll get to it eventually" projects and a large workshop you could see from the road where he made his living building custom furniture, I actually for the first time since starting this never-ending game with karma, and those once prescribed pills was at ease. I don't know if it was because I was finally taking the first steps to start over or the warm pizza that was sitting on my lap during then, no one said a word ride over to my brother's place since I hadn't eaten anything in a day or so. Either way, it would be the calm before the storm that I wasn't at all ready for.

One of the most popular not at all true opinions about addicts is that they keep using to get high so they can forget their problems as if being homeless and/or hungry while hoping tomorrow doesn't come is a problem you can simply forget about. No, the biggest reason addicts continue a relationship with their drug of choice has nothing to do with getting high, but more about not getting sick! Detoxing is often compared to having a nasty case of the "flu," but that's like comparing the picture of what a hamburger is supposed to look like on the menu of any fast-food restaurant and what the kid actually hands you—not even close!

Unlike the flu that offers many over-the-counter remedies that can be bought at millions of stores anywhere, with withdrawal from opiates, the only treatment available is to ride out the hell that my addiction caused while second-guessing if tomorrow was worth seeing, all the way up to the first click of my first failed attempt to make sure I didn't, as if someone thought I was worth more than zero, but I knew it was merely karma's way of saying, "I'm not done yet."

After unpacking the small bag of "everything I had left" in my new residence that was an old couch in my brother's basement, we both sat down together, ate the pizza that had been resting on my lap during the ride there, and talked about everything from "remember when we were kids," the latest stupid things people do, along with very specific ground rules for my stay there. The first one being that he was okay with me working off the cost of my visit, the second was that the workday starts at 6:00 a.m., basically everything except the reason I was there.

I spent my first sleepless night trapped in the safest most dangerous place I knew—my head! listening to karma play my greatest regrets over and over while counting the minutes of my sobriety, using old TV shows for a timer as my body continued to send me less-than-subtle hints that it was long overdue for those once-prescribed pills, and if I thought the cold sweats and insomnia was terrible, just wait, it only gets worse.

The sun had just barely started shining through the one small window available at my current residence when I decided that it was early enough for me to get a shower and wash away any evidence that I had spent the whole night crying before my brother woke up, but as I slowly made my way up the stairs into the kitchen, I could see the shadow of him, drinking a cup of his high-octane coffee through the window over the sink full of "I'll wash them when I need them" dishes, and beside him, a cup with the steam rising off it, letting me know he wanted me to join him without saying a word.

I used what little bit of the "no energy" I had left and made my way to the chair next to the cup of coffee my brother had waiting for me, hoping to catch some of the secondhand smoke from the cigarette he was smoking since my last one had been rationed down to nothing the sleepless night before, and maybe warm my cold sweaty hands a bit on the cup of coffee since drinking it would just irritate the withdrawal symptoms that were becoming stronger while trying to come up with answers to the twenty questions I just knew he was going to ask, but instead he only asked one.

"Do you know what makes sunrises awesome?"

A little more than frustrated since it wasn't a question, I had prepared myself for and never really did good in science from kindergarten to graduation, I quickly answered, "No, but I'm sure you're going to tell me."

Preparing for what I thought would be one of those long scientific answers my brother always liked to give, I was a little more than surprised when he answered with just a single word, "Consistency." He then explained, "You see, no matter what's going on in our own little world whether it's, good, bad, we're alive, or dead, that sun is going to come up, and the only thing that is just as consistent as that sun is shit happens! It doesn't matter if you're a good person, bad person, it's self-inflicted or no fault of your own, shit will happen. The key to surviving those consistent sunrises is to simply make sure you know where your shoes are, so you don't get any of that shit between your toes."

He took one more drink of his coffee and headed to the workshop in the backyard to get things ready for my first day of work, but not before passing me a cigarette I could enjoy while reflecting on what he had just told me but my mind was at the place I once called home with, Marie.

Now you might be looking for the inspirational part of this story like in those rocky movies when the music starts to play, and you see him working his way to another win, but as it says in the title, this story is "semiautobiographical," and I was in no shape to do anything more than drag myself to that long-anticipated shower to wash the smell off burnt bologna and regret off. Before making my way to the workshop, where my brother had a small little fifteen-minute job for me to do that would take the next eight hours or so to complete because of the frequent trips to the bathroom to throw up things I hadn't eaten or to sit on the toilet since I was finally able to do what I couldn't do as one of the side effects of opiate use.

After a long day of doing as much as my body would let me, I dined on some saltine crackers and water because of the standoff I was in with my body over the lack of those pills it had become accustomed to over the past three years, followed by another sleepless night trapped in my head where karma made sure that every thought was about Marie and the little things that she did that made me fall in love with her again and again. Things like the way her smile made everything ok no matter how bad it was, how my shirt was always her favorite PJs, or when I would pretend to fall asleep on the couch just to get that soft kiss on my forehead before she made her way to bed, all while trying to block out the sound of the quickly becoming regular voices in my head that were laughing out loud at what I had become.

It would take about sixty-eight hours of sobriety before my body would finally let my top and bottom eyelids get reacquainted for a couple of hours or so before waking me up just in time to enjoy the cold sweats, body aches, along with the continuing anticipation that Marie might finally respond to one of the many "I'm sorry, I love you" and "Are you okay" texts I had been sending since the start of the end of my world. Strengthening my belief that Marie no longer wanted me to be part of her life, and that tomorrow's consistent sunrise would be just another thing better without me.

My brother must have noticed that I had become a little more than comfortable with the idea of ending my tomorrows because he decided to join me on the roof, where I was supposed to be cleaning gutters but instead was trying to figure out if there was enough distance between me and the ground to end my life, or would the fall simply cripple me enough to be more of a burden to anyone else.

After climbing the old rickety ladder I was using, since personal safety wasn't one of my primary concerns at that time, and onto the roof where I had been doing my calculations instead of everything else he asked me to do. My brother took a quick look around before sitting down close enough to the edge of the roof for his feet to dangle off, took two cigarettes from the almost empty pack he had in the front shirt pocket of the plain T-shirt he was wearing, letting me know that we needed to talk, whether I wanted to or not.

I hesitantly made my way to the spot my brother had reserved for me while quietly rehearsing the several lies I planned on telling him about why nothing he asked me to do on the roof was done in my head, sat down, took the cigarette he had waiting for me, and prepared myself for a game of twenty questions that turned out to only have one direct one.

"Why are you doing this?"

I immediately answered, "To get things back to the way they were, to be with Marie," and with that same Southern boy smirk that I had seen on my father's face many times before, my brother quickly replied, "If you think this hell you are going through will somehow change things back to the way they were, you're a bigger idiot than I ever gave you credit for. Forget about the past because tomorrow has no time for it! What's done is done, and as for doing it for Marie, you need to get your priorities straight, little brother. The only person you need to do this for is you, not Marie, not your kids, just you! Because whether you're using or sober, you will always be an addict to them no matter how much you try to prove otherwise, so make peace with it.". He then passed me another cigarette from the now empty pack before heading back to the whatever he was doing in the workshop and as I watched him make his way down off the roof using the old rickety ladder instead of my gravity technique, I realized two things: the first was that he was right, the second, he was a lot smarter than any of his report cards ever gave him credit for, proving that Einstein's whole fish and everyone's a genius theory was right.

It would take three weeks, two sets of bunk beds, and one dining room table, followed by several hours of coffee cup counseling and workshop philosophy provided by my older brother before I would start to feel a little like the person I was before the so-called accidental run-in with Helen's SUV. All the tantrums my body had been throwing for those once-prescribed pills, along with the every minute or so text messages I had been sending Marie to let her know I was okay, even though I was pretty confident that she didn't care one way or another, were now every other day or so apart. My clothes fit a lot looser around the waist than they did at the beginning of my unconventional rehab since I still couldn't hold down much more than crackers, and the sleepless nights I usually spent trapped inside my head, where the voices continuously reminded of everything I lost due to my addiction, were now being interrupted by random four-hour visits from the sandman.

Unlike my sleeping habits, my days had become routine as routine could be, considering my current circumstances. I would start each day with a long hot shower in an attempt to quiet the voices in my head that just didn't seem to want to go away, get dressed in the cleanest of the few clothes I had left, then join my brother on the back porch, where I first learned about those always consistent sunrises for several cups of his high-octane coffee that my body had somehow become used to while we discussed the list of things he would appreciate I do that day. Until one morning, instead of finding my brother on the back porch, I found a fresh pack of smokes with a note stuck to them that read, "I have a few important errands to run. Enjoy the smokes, mow the yard, and I'll be back a little later," followed by the exact location of where I could find the key to his new mower, a half-full gas can in case I ran out, and which part of the yard I was to stay out of so his mower wouldn't get stuck.

After finishing a cup of my brother's high-octane coffee and two chain-smoked cigarettes from the fresh pack he left for me, I headed out to where my brother's note said I would find the keys and gas for his new lawn mower to begin the physical therapy part of my unconventional rehab, deciding it would be best to start in the front part of the yard and work my way to the back, where the spot my brother's note warned me about was.

Now I'm not sure if it was the music I was listening to way above the normal volume level to drown out the voices in my head or that I was a little too impressed with myself for finishing the front part of the yard without being interrupted by nausea, cold sweats, or having to run to the bathroom that distracted me just long enough to land my brother's new mower in the exact spot he had explicitly told me to stay away from leaving me tire deep in the mud and stuck.

In a panic, I quickly jumped off the now-sinking mower and began rocking it back and forth with the little bit of strength I had in an attempt to break it free from the hole it was sinking in, but all I managed to accomplish was making the situation a lot worse than it was. After screaming few choice four-letter words to whoever wasn't there listening and a small childlike temper fit, I came up with the not-so-bright idea to put my brother's new mower in gear, get behind it, and push, thinking I should be able to catch the unmanned mower after it broke free from the mudhole with no trouble at all.

Now as good as that plan sounded in my head, I don't think I need to tell you it wasn't. Instead, what happened was the lawn mower broke loose, and I fell face-first into the mudhole I had just made, covering me from head to toe, but not before the pants that were now two or more sizes too big on me fell safely around my ankles, exposing that Marie may have forgotten to pack any underwear in the small green bag she had left for me on the porch the day I began my recovery, not to mention the only thing that caught the runaway mower was the back wall of my brother's workshop, causing it to stall just in time for me to hear my brother laugh harder than I had ever heard him laugh before over the spectacle I had just made of myself.

After pulling up my shorts that were now resting comfortably around my ankles, exposing parts of me that most have never seen and wiping some of the mud from my eyes, I quickly turned to where the sound of my brother's laughter was coming from to give him one of those "Really, you thought it was funny" looks when I noticed there standing beside him was Marie. Still beautiful beyond my reach with her shoulder-length strawberry-blond hair that was now highlighted in gray, her crystal-blue eyes with a lot of tired behind them, and her smile that somehow made me believe tomorrow had a purpose and just like when I met her the summer before my senior year of high school, I was at a loss for words even though I had practiced what I might say over and over in my head during one of my many sleepless nights battling addiction.

Still not completely convinced that it was Marie standing there beside my brother and not just some figment of my imagination brought to me by karma, I began wiping more of the mud from my eyes while I walked toward the sound of my brother's laughter where Marie met me halfway, put her arms around me the same way she did every time I arrived home from work, and said, "Hey, baby, you didn't forget date night, did you?" leaving every reason I was at my brother's, something we would talk about whenever.

We spent our first date night in forever sitting on the back porch, where I usually had my coffee cup counseling sessions at, holding hands like we hadn't done in way too long as we listened to my brother tell several different "If you thought the whole lawn mower thing was funny, wait until you hear this one" stories from the past several weeks of my recovery while he cooked a bachelor's feast of frozen hamburger patties to be served with several different types of not-quite-stale bags of potato chips that were just taking up space on the kitchen counter. The hours we spent together seemed to pass by in seconds, and before I knew it, the moon had already replaced that day's always-consistent sunrise in the sky, leaving me to wonder where I might be spending that sleepless night at.

With all the dirty dishes from the hamburger and stale potato chip feast, my brother cooked for us safely in the sink with all the other "I'll wash them when I need them" dishes and the last "did he ever tell you about the time we did this" story from long before my addiction told. I decided that it was time for me to finally ask Marie the question of where I would be spending that night even though I was scared of what her answer might be. I spent the next few minutes or so in the privacy of my head, quietly rehearsing exactly how I would ask Marie such a difficult question when all the sudden my brother blurted out, "So is he staying here or going with you?" in which Marie quickly replied, "He's coming with me," followed by a soft kiss on my cheek. My brother took a quick drag off the cigarette he was smoking, looked over at me, and said, "Good, go get your shit out of my basement. I have to get some sleep since some of us here have a busy day tomorrow," followed by the same smirk I had seen on my father's face many times before letting me know he was happy for me without saying a word.

I have called my brother many things of the years some nice, some not so nice, but that night, for the first time, I realized that even though he didn't wear a cape, my brother was my hero.

Chapter 4

Welcome Home

WE OFTEN USE the phrase baby steps, to describe the small steps it usually takes to complete the long challenges that are required to get through those always consistent sunrises my brother had told me about a little over three weeks ago when I first made the awkward phone call to him after reading the note of so few words but said so much that Marie had left for me. These are the same kind of steps karma would use to test the strengths of my recovery, along with what little bit of sanity I may have had left.

With what little I had left, packed not so neatly in the same bag Marie left for me on the porch of my soon-to-be new residence in the back seat of the unfamiliar car Marie was driving since the bank had recently reposed the fancier previous model I bought her for on Valentine's Day a couple of years before due to lack of payment, I watched as Marie kissed my brother on the cheek and whispered something I'm still not sure what in his ear before taking my place in the passenger seat for the much-anticipated and dreaded drive to my first full day of starting over without my brother there to guide me through each step.

During the few mile ride from my brother's place to the house Marie fell in love with twenty-some-odd years ago after reading the ad that seemed to be written just for us. No one said a word except for the guy on the radio who was letting us know about the slight chance of rain that was already hitting the passenger window I was looking out of watching the streetlights pass by, hoping Marie wouldn't ask the one question I had no answer to—"Why?"—while trying to kick the feeling that the game karma invited me to play wasn't over.

After we pulled into the driveway, that was now outlined by not-so-freshly trimmed hedges, Marie put our brand-new clunker in park, turned the ignition to the off position, and looked at me with the same smile that lit up the loading docks I was standing on the night we first met the summer before my senior year of high school, and said, "We're home," finally breaking the silence that started at the end of my brother's driveway.

As I watched Marie push more than a couple of times on the old rusty door of our new more-than-slightly used car open and start making her way down the stone walkway, passed the big bay window, and to the "not so freshly painted" brown door, where Patty was waiting for us the first time we looked at the house we would raise our family in. I began looking through all the gunk-covered windows starting with the passenger side to see who wasn't there laughing at me in perfect harmony with the voices in my head that had been taunting me since my first night of recovery over what I had become, hoping maybe to catch quick a glimpse of the silver lining that is supposed to appear after my little victory over those once-prescribed pills. But the only silver I saw was on a brand-new Mercedes, complete with personalized plates that read "Her Baby" sitting in the Jones's driveway, leaving me to wonder if I could even compete anymore in the unspoken contest that had been going on between Mr. Jones and me all these years. After all, if anyone deserved everything, it was Marie.

With the coast clear of any imaginary onlookers, I grabbed the "not so neatly packed" bag Marie left for me the day I began my "unconventional rehab" from the back seat of the rust-covered car we were now proud owners of and began making my way down the stone walkway, passed the big bay window to the now open brown door, where Marie was waving for me to join her inside. Once inside, I sat the bag in the same place by the door we always left our shoes, boots, and coats at, making sure to leave it "not so neatly packed" just in case my return home didn't turn out quite like I had imagined every sleepless night at my brother's house and I would have to leave quickly.

Still not completely convinced of Marie's welcome, I stood by the open door for a couple of minutes or more looking around at all the several changes that had taken place in the past couple of weeks or so I spent battling my addiction. Before taking those baby steps we talked about at the beginning of this chapter through the now empty dining room since the table we used to have our "How was your day" dinners at was the last thing I sold before Marie had drawn her line in the sand and to the bar, or "peninsula" as Patty liked to call it, where the youngest of our two sons, Austin, was waiting with a fresh cup of "not nearly as strong as my brother's" coffee and an unopened pack of my brand cigarettes beside him, ending the confusion of where my next smoke might come from since I was pretty sure my older brother boosted my last pack like he's done for years.

All the custom furniture Marie picked to match the rest of the house has been replaced by several secondhand pieces that didn't even match each other, let alone anything else, and the high-end TV that was now at the local pawnshop where I had sold it has since been replaced by one of those older models that usually required two people to move—courtesy of "I have no idea who." On the stone fireplace were Marie kept all the pictures of events I was too busy working to be part of now had several newly scalped Facebook pictures of our two grandsons that we have never met since our oldest son thought it was best to keep them away from an addict, along with anyone who supported them.

Making sure to keep my head in the down position like I was checking to see if my slip-on shoes were untied, I carefully pulled out the barstool closest to the still-open door, sat down, and prepared to "explain myself" the same way my grandpa always asked me to do when I may or may not have made a mistake or two. A few minutes of awkward silence passed when my youngest son looked at me with the same cocky smirk I had seen on my dad's face many times before and asked, "What, did you quit smoking too?" causing me and the voices in my head that had been quiet until then to giggle just a little.

The next several hours, I spent listening to Marie and my youngest son talk about things like "Dad, do you remember that time we…" and how the first night I met Marie, she somehow knew in just that few minutes we spoke that she wanted to spend the rest of her life with me while chain-smoking several cigarettes from the pack my youngest son had waiting for me on the bar where I used to serve my special dad's home pan-sized pancakes at, impatiently waiting for someone to mention the elephant in the room—that was my addiction, but surprisingly, no one did.

My son ended our trip down memory lane by announcing that it was time for him to go to bed since he had to work a "split shift" the next day at the local sandwich shop, where he and Marie got jobs to keep up the appearance that everything was "okay" while hiding their secret shame that was me. With my son in his room on the second floor, Marie slowly walked over to where I was sitting, put her arms around my neck, the same way she did when I carried her over the threshold of her parents' house the day we got married, and with the look of "Everything's going to be okay" in her eyes, asked if I was ready for bed while leading me upstairs to the room we shared together for the past twenty-some-odd years as if I had any other choice but to follow.

Once we made it to the top of the stairs and into the privacy of our room, Marie and I began dancing slowly to our song about "If You're Serious" that she was humming softly in my ear just like she did on those late nights she would sneak over via the soccer fields next to my parents' house to spend the night with me in the clubhouse my dad built for us when we were kids. We made it all the way to the last verse of the song when Marie excused herself to, as she put it, "slip into something more comfortable." While Marie was away I sat uncomfortably down on the edge of the bed and began to dry my sweaty palms that I had been hiding from her since the first steps of our couple's only dance, on the unfamiliar comforter that wasn't nearly as soft as the fancier ones we had before. A few minutes passed by in what felt like hours when Marie suddenly appeared wearing the sexiest thing I had ever seen her wear—my shirt—leaving me speechless just like when we first met the summer before my senior year of high school. After getting a little more reacquainted with each other since my coming home, Marie and I climbed under the covers, where she took her favorite sleeping position, and as I felt her "always a little bit cold" nose pressed against my chest and her arms around the much smaller me, I mistakenly put the idea of karma still stalking me to the furthest part of my mind until my usual 3:00 a.m. wake-up call brought on by the recurring nightmares I regularly have now about all the things I had done chasing those once-prescribed pills.

Careful not to disturb Marie from what looked like a pretty peaceful night's sleep, I slowly climbed out of bed and staggered my way into the bathroom for a long hot shower in an attempt to lower the tone of the voices in my head, making sure the large mirror on the wall above the sink was steamed covered so I wouldn't have to look myself in the face since I couldn't stand the sight of me. With the first of my now several showers a day was over and the tone of voices in my head at a tolerable level, I stood quietly in the doorway of our room, watching Marie sleep until that day's consistent sunrise began shining through the frost-covered window she likes to keep open on those brisk fall nights, hoping her dreams were not only better than my usual nightmares but that I was in some way part of them.

Felling like this day couldn't get any more perfect, which should have been my first clue that karma wasn't done with me and was only making plans for worse things to come, I decided to start my new daily routine of drinking coffee, and smoking cigarettes, while having a one-sided conversation with the voices in my head, instead of my overly confident brother, on the back deck, where once a year Marie used to leave a big bag of Christmas toys for the boys that I would later distribute in my best dressed Santa suit.

Once outside, I spent a few minutes looking around to see if I could put a face with the voices that were now debating with me over how things were going with Marie before taking a seat in one of the old patio chairs located at the furthest side of the deck and out of range of any prying ears that may or may not be listening to me, mumbling things to myself. I had just started on my second cup of morning coffee and a third cigarette when my youngest son, Austin, decided to join me, carrying his unusual breakfast of whatever leftovers were available from the night before and one of those types of drinks that are supposed to give you wings to help him get through the first part of his split shift that was set to start shortly.

Several moments of silence passed before I somehow found the courage to mumble in between sips of coffee, "I'm sorry," finally being the first to talk about what I hoped would simply be tucked away in the book of things we don't talk about anymore. My son took a quick drink to help him swallow the mouthful of something or another he was eating and looked at me and asked, "For what? Did you fart?" which was just his way of saying, "It's okay. We all make mistakes."

Over the next week or so, I spent my days trying to become an overachiever at everything I neglected to do during my pill-chasing days—from trimming those hedges that lined the driveway to cooking fancy dinners that my youngest son, Austin, described simply as an acquired taste. My nights, on the other hand, were usually spent in the living room where Marie and I usually had our date nights at, sitting in the dark, watching late-night infomercials about protecting your identity while quietly conversing with the voices in my head that were still suggesting that tomorrow's consistent sunrise doesn't require me to see it.

I didn't have many visitors, just my older brother who was checking up on me like any good doctor without a degree would, Lennie, who was making sure I was still giving him a ride home to his bachelor pad that was located in his parents' basement. After our annual birthday smoke session, since his car would be at the mechanics, getting more than a couple of things fixed and, of course, Mr. Jones's wife, Kim, who, I'm pretty sure, was just visiting so she could gather up enough gossip to give everyone in the neighborhood something to talk about for the next however long or so.

I have to admit, I was pretty impressed with the way Marie handled all Kim's questions about where all the high-end stuff I sold, feeding my addiction, went, telling her that everything was in one of those storage units I didn't know we had so it wouldn't get damaged during the up-and-coming remodel I didn't know was going to take place since everyone knows how clumsy the contractors I didn't know we hired can be. Leaving Kim with nothing to talk about with anyone in the neighborhood and a little jealous, I wasn't sure if Marie told Kim the well-thought-out lie to save herself from the embarrassment that I obviously caused. Or that she was in her own way, letting me know she had already forgiven me for everything I had done without me having to ask for it. Keeping "what's done is done" exactly where my older brother recommended, we keep it, in the past.

With just a little over six hours left of my thirty-ninth year on this earth, and twice as many before I would hear the guy on the radio tell me the lie about how "It's going to be a beautiful day," I decided to get things ready for my first day back to my home away from home at the dealership where the prices are the lowest around and everyone drives, even those with less-than-perfect credit. I started by ironing all the recently purchased secondhand clothes that Marie and I spent a day together shopping for since my older ones no longer fit the much smaller me and finished with picking out a tie that had the least amount of stains on it. After everything was pressed, polished, and picked, I joined Marie, Austin, and Lennie on the back porch for several of those "do you remember the time we" stories from long before my addiction and the first meal I had eaten in a month or so that didn't consist of just crackers.

I'm not quite sure how I missed all of karma's subtle hints that the game between us was far from over. It may have been because of the way Marie was looking at me with those crystal-blue eyes while I laughed at several of the stories Lennie was telling about why he's still a bachelor or that the voices in my head had been quiet for the last day or so; either way, I was about to get schooled in the most difficult subject ever—life—that would eventually lead to me lying on the street, looking up at an unfamiliar face that claimed I was stable.

Chapter 5

Miss Me Yet

DIVERSION IS OFTEN defined as an activity that distracts us from any and all serious concerns, or as my dad would say, "Magic isn't real, the diversion is," which would explain how karma was able to sneak all her well-planned accidental events that would forever change the course of those consistent sunrises my brother had told me about just a little over four weeks ago.

With Marie's sexy man lie told and the new "Number 1 Dad" travel mug my youngest son, Austin, bought for me as an early birthday present the day before at the dollar store in hand, I walked outside to the passenger side of our new unfamiliar clunker and began to check, double-check, and check again, making sure I didn't forget anything I might need for my first day back to my prison with a paycheck at the dealership since I was pretty sure all eyes would be watching my every move, patiently waiting for me to slip back to the person I said goodbye to the first night of my unconventional rehab. Starting with my recently pinched butt, I tapped it twice to make sure I had the empty wallet I still carry since it belonged to my dad then wound the watch I would spend most of the day looking at as it took hours for the minutes to tick by. I even had Marie text me a friendly reminder that Lennie would need a ride home after our annual birthday "Smoke Session" that we had been doing since we met twenty-plus birthdays ago at one of the many fast-food restaurants I worked at before landing the cushy job at my dad's place. Even with all the "check, double-check, and check again" effort I put into making sure I had everything I would need that day, I still somehow managed to completely overlook the game karma made me an unwilling participant in moments after my so-called accidental run-in with Helen's SUV that was set to resume seconds after my final wave goodbye to Marie, and the sound of the door located between the showroom and body shop that she dropped me off in front of clicking closed behind me.

Once inside, and out of the chilly rain that was starting to fall, I quickly ducked into the bathroom, which was located next to the vending machines I usually ate my breakfast, lunch, and dinner from for a few deep breaths, and a quick once-over to make sure that my new secondhand clothes didn't get wrinkled on the ride there. With my slightly stained tie, I picked out the night before straight and my confidence as good as it's ever going to get. I stepped out of the bathroom and began heading to the office where I spent most of my and Marie's twenty-some-odd years of marriage at working, which was now being occupied by a someone or another who wasn't me, causing the voices that had been quiet for the past day or so to break out in laughter like I never heard before.

I took a few steps closer so I could maybe identify the somebody I was about to enforce the move-it-or-lose-it rule on. When I noticed just outside the same door, Helen had been taping her Lee Press-On Nails against the day. This nightmare I can't seem to wake up from started with was a banker's style box with my last name written on it, followed by in big bold letters the word "junk."

With what little bit of confidence I may or may not have had gone, I stood quietly outside the same office where this somebody was resting his feet on my old desk, looking at all the places where every picture Marie ever framed for me once hung that had since been replaced by certificates of completion, posing as diplomas with the well-known secret's name Matt wrote on them, confirming that the game karma made me an unwilling participant in was far from over, and this was just the first of many well-planned accidental events still to come.

Matt wasn't a bad kid, he wasn't the smartest either, but I guess you don't need intelligence if there is a good chance that you were the result of one of my bosses' many "Sorry, honey, I'm working late at the dealership" nights that were spent with the aftermarket girl on the same desk he was currently sitting behind. Everyone at the dealership knew about the affair, everyone except my boss's wife and the sharp as a marble Matt, of course.

Now mad as hell, I calmly placed my new "No. 1 Dad" travel mug on the box that had my last name written on it in big bold letters and began rolling up the sleeves of my new second shirt while rehearsing the few choice words I was going to say to Matt during the hands-on confrontation that would be written about in the police report I just knew would be filed. When in a saved-by-the-bell moment, my boss paged over the loudspeaker, "All salesman, sales desk," signaling that it was time for our usual 9:00 a.m. sales meeting, where we discussed what was going on with any and all pending deals. In an attempt to make sure my not-at-all-happy face was the first thing my boss seen when he started to take attendance, I pushed my way through all the salesmen that were beginning to gather around the sales desk to the spot directly in front of him, hoping to apply a little pressure for him to explain to me what exactly took place during my so-called "vacation" while letting him know that no matter what it was, I was in no way happy about it.

After the sales, meeting ended, and everyone went to their respective offices, except for me, since I had no idea where my office was anymore. I just stood staring at my boss, looking for some kind of answer that I was sure wouldn't be good enough for how mad I was at that moment. Knowing that I was in no way going to walk away quietly if I didn't get some answers, my boss picked up his phone, called the operator, and told her to hold all his calls like he always did before having a sit-down with any employee. With all his calls being held, my boss signaled for me to follow him to the empty office next to my old one where the aftermarket girl, and Matt's mom, would do as little as possible and still get paid for it.

He started the conversation, saying, "I meant to give you heads-up on all this"—like for some reason, every phone in the place suddenly didn't work in my absence, and he couldn't give me a call or that I had traveled to a place so exotic that they didn't have phones, which would have been impossible with my current financial situation that he knew about; after all, he signed my paycheck.

I listened for the next "I have no idea" minutes, as my boss explained all the reasons, why he did, what he did. The first being that the relationship and trust with the banks that we had worked with all those forever years had become questionable since my addiction started, followed by several other reasons I didn't listen to because I was trying to figure how could I explain this to Marie or if I would even tell her at all. Keeping this one little secret to myself until I could figure out a way to rebuild everything I wrecked for my addiction to those once prescribed pills, on what would amount to a little less than half what I had been getting paid before. My boss ended our meeting by saying, "I hope there are no hard feelings" while holding out his hand for me to shake as if I would just understand that it wasn't "nothing personal just business" even though to me, it was everything.

I hesitantly shook his hand, and we parted ways—him to the front desk that we called "The Tower" and me to the same spot that I was standing when Helen's SUV pinned me against the wall, to chain-smoke several cigarettes from one of the two packs Austin had been buying for the "still broke" me—while trying to convince myself that the real reason Matt replaced me after my nearly twenty years of dedication to the dealership was because of the well-known secret instead of the real reasons my boss just told me.

I finished the last of three cigarettes I had been chain-smoking before picking up the box marked with big bold letters that spelled my last name, followed by the word "junk" karma used to remind me that our little game was far from over and moved it into my new office that was located directly behind the same one I had occupied for years. That was just an old storage room and final resting place for old phones, brochures of old cars from ten years before, and an old broken desk with an even older computer on it that I would use to maintain the dealership's website that I didn't know we had, let alone how to maintain it for my new position of internet manager.

Realizing that any hope of redeeming myself to Marie was slowly but surely slipping away, I placed the dust-covered banker's style box strategically on the corner of the old broken down desk just in case anyone walked in on me to find out where I had been all this time, they wouldn't see the tears that were starting to form in the corners of my eyes before beginning their journey down my face.

I spent the next several minutes or so asking the now-quite-vocal voices in my head "Why this was happening to me?" even though I already knew the answer. When I heard my last name announced over the loudspeaker, letting me know that I had a call waiting for me on line 3, I cleared my throat and dried the tears that had been falling before answering with my best fake "This is… How can I help you" just in case it was Marie calling since I didn't want her to hear the sound of everything's not okay in my voice. A few seconds of silence passed before I heard the sound of my overly confident brother's voice singing a really bad version of the "Happy Birthday" song.

After my brother's horrible performance, I did my best impression of laughter, hoping he wouldn't figure out that I was starting to hate those consistent sunrises he spoke so highly of at the start of my unconventional rehab. My impression must have been just as bad as his performance of the "Happy Birthday" song since the next words out of his mouth was "How are you handling things back in the real world?"

Making sure my answer was a perfectly worded lie since I didn't have the heart to tell him that I would much rather be the guy people are talking about when they say, "Do you remember the time he…?" I told my brother everything was perfect and that it couldn't get any better, hopefully sparing him the burden of ever thinking that he could have done more when more wasn't possible. We talked for a few more minutes about things that probably wouldn't make sense to anyone else but us before hanging up and getting back to the misery I would have to spend the next twelve hours stuck in.

I spent the rest of the day that wouldn't end, trying to make my new "closet-size" office somewhat clean and functional by throwing away all the outdated lunch menus that had accumulated in the old letter trays that were on top of my only available filing cabinet, replacing them with what looked like important papers that actually meant nothing at all, followed by going through every drawer, throwing away broken paperclips, pens that didn't write, and all the nicely packaged plastic silverware/

napkin combos, that seemed to be in every drawer by the hundreds all in an effort to dodge contact with anyone that might ask how my so-called vacation was or how I lost so much weight in such a short time.

With my new office as clean as it could be and only the last half of the twelve-hour day left, I cautiously stepped out of my rabbit hole located right behind my old office that was now being occupied by the well-known secret Matt to find out what car I would be using as a demo for the long drive home when I accidentally ran into my first customer in my new position by the name of Joe Jackson.

At just a few inches short of being six-foot-tall Joe, or Mr. Jackson as he preferred to be called, showed up that night, wearing what could only be described as something straight from a 1980s Sears and Roebuck catalog, smelling like Johnny Walker, burned bologna, and regret. He managed to stagger a couple of steps into the showroom before introducing himself in the worst way any customer could, asking, "Who wants to sell me a car?" immediately clearing the showroom of any salesman, except for me, of course.

Positive my boss was watching my every move, I hesitantly made the effort to introduce myself to Joe, followed by the question, "And you are?" He quickly replied with the kind of accent that told me he's eaten a SPAM sandwich or two, "My name is Joseph, Joseph Jackson, all my friends call me Joe, but you can call me Mr. Jackson." He then explained that he was a little more than interested in the Mustang that was sitting on the new car lot under several spotlights. Now, this wasn't just your average Mustang but a 650 horsepower GT500 in the always popular "grabber blue" and trimmed in the legendary white Shelby stripes.

The dealership had many rules, but only two were ever really enforced. The first being that if you thought for even a second that the customer might have been drinking, or in any way impaired, don't let them drive anything. Second, make sure that the customer was even qualified to buy such a specialty car like that Mustang before putting the miles on it. Which if you based Mr. Jackson's qualifications solely on the way he looked, and the barely running nineties something black truck with brown replacement panels, he drove up in, I would probably say he didn't.

Acting purely out of frustration over all the valid reasons my boss gave me earlier that day on why I was demoted, along with knowing that as long as I was there, Matt would have to be there too. I decided to use the "never judge a book by its cover" rule, grabbed the keys, and a dealer tag, before crossing the not-so-busy street that divided the new car lot from the showroom with Mr. Jackson staggering closely behind. As we were crossing the street, I began asking Mr. Jackson the standard small talk questions like, "What do you do for a living? Are you married? Or have any kids?" And with a harsh tone in his voice, Mr. Jackson quickly answered each question in the exact order, I had asked them, "Retired, temporarily separated, and from time to time" leading me to believe that he wasn't one of those friendly talkative types.

Once on the new car lot and out of my boss's line of sight, I unlocked the 650 horsepower GT500 Mustang with the remote I was carrying and began doing my best "walk around" presentation, making sure to show Mr. Jackson all the fancy options that he just didn't seem to care about. After my far-from-perfect "walk around" since I haven't had to do one in forever or so, I handed Mr. Jackson the keys and watched as he made himself right at home in the driver's seat before asking if it was okay for him to, as he put it, "start her up," a request I was more than happy to grant. Mr. Jackson made a few more adjustments to the driver's seat he was sitting in then placed the key in the ignition, turning it just enough to bring those 650 ponies to life and for the first time since we meet just a few minutes before a smile to his old and tired face.

Feeling like there's no better time than the present, I asked Mr. Jackson if he was ready to take his free test drive—since everything else on the lot would cost him somewhere between fifty and sixty thousand, he might as well take advantage of the free stuff!—causing him to quickly turn the ignition to the off position, hand me the keys, and with the same expression on his face I had seen somewhere before, saying, "Son, I'm a little drunk, not a whole lot crazy. I'll drive it when I take her home. So let's go inside so you can do whatever it is you need to do to make that happen," something I quickly agreed to.

With the keys now safely in my possession, and Mr. Jackson slowly staggering behind me, mumbling out loud to someone that wasn't there, "A promise is a promise. A deal's a deal," we crossed the not-at-all-busy street to the showroom to begin the process of making Mr. Jackson the proud owner of the rare 650-horsepower GT500 Mustang in the always-popular "grabber blue," trimmed with white Shelby stripes.

Once inside and out of the chilly night air, we sat down in one of the many empty offices, since everyone else was already at home for the day, and I began filling out all the paperwork required when purchasing any car, truck, or SUV while Mr. Jackson told the story of how he picked up his wife of many years for their first official date in the same kind of Mustang I was hoping to sell him that night, except his was a different color and a lot older, of course, chuckling when he got to the part of how he had to park down the street from her parents' house since he wasn't at all what her dad wanted for his daughter.

After filling in all the blanks on the required paperwork with Mr. Jackson's name, address, and phone number, along with the five-figure amount it was going to cost to own the rare Mustang, I turned the buyer's order around and asked Mr. Jackson for his signature right next to the X I circled on the purchaser's signature line and a deposit to hold the Mustang until whenever he planned on picking it up.

Careful not to break the cardinal rule in sales that clearly states the first one who speaks loses, I sat quietly and watched as Mr. Jackson pulled an old pair of reading glasses from the inside pocket of the black-and-white flannel coat he was wearing, place them on his face, and begin checking that all the information I had written down was correct, including the price of the Mustang, before signing his name in the exact spot I had marked with a circled X, completing my first sale as the new internet manager, except for the deposit, of course.

Not wanting to jeopardize the sort of friendly relationship Mr. Jackson and I had developed in the past couple of hours or so after closing, I decided instead of asking him for the required deposit that I would just take the last and only ten-dollar bill I had from the hiding spot in my wallet and use it instead. I'm not sure why I did it, maybe I just wanted a valid reason to give Marie on why I was late again that could be verified by my name and 2013 GT500 written on the sales for the day window in white shoe polish or that, for some reason I'm still not sure about, I trusted Mr. Jackson like he was an old friend from my past that I had somehow forgotten about.

Now I know what you're thinking, this is like one of those Oscar-nominated moments where I say something like, "As strange as it sounds, my addiction was the best thing that could have happened to me because it taught me something or another," followed by the semi sad song, ending credits, and still photos of how great things turned out. Well, you would be wrong. There were no ending credits, no still photos, and as for the sad song, it was more like that song about a highway you took to hell, and karma was driving.

Chapter 6

So, I Was Thinking

"STOP AND THINK before you do it" is a phrase my dad always said to me, usually after I did something that he referred to as "dumb" or "stupid" and exactly what I should have done before using my last ten dollars as a deposit on Mr. Jackson's recent purchase that he probably won't remember buying once he sobered up, starting round two of the game karma invited me to play the day Helen pinned me against the wall with her five-month-old SUV.

With Mr. Jackson's deal signed, sealed, and scheduled to be picked up the upcoming Friday, I stood outside the dealership for a minute or two and watched as the taillights of Mr. Jackson's "barely running" truck disappearing into the night before going inside to grab the strategically placed box with my name written on it in big bold letters followed by the word "junk" from my desk and the keys to the car Matt picked for me to drive home that was just as you might expect it to be, above the "E" that didn't stand for enough.

After a few shallow congratulations from my boss and the well-known secret Matt for making the "if come maybe" sale to Mr. Jackson that only cost me my last ten dollars, I carefully placed the box that contained every picture Marie had framed for me over the years in the front passenger seat of the car I was sure Matt picked for me because of the lack of fuel in it and began the what "seemed like forever" white-knuckled drive home, stopping only twice. Once for a friendly officer who, for my birthday, let me off with a warning for exceeding the posted speed limit in an attempt to get home a little less late than I already was. The second to give the Jones's place a not-so-friendly read-between-the-lines-type salute where I noticed that the car parked in Mr. Jones's normal parking spot wasn't even his.

Once on the street Marie and I raised our two boys on for the past twenty-some-odd years and safe from running out of gas far from walking distance, I started to feel just a little too confident in my thoughts, that the worst was behind me and began enjoying how peaceful our street was at that hour, unlike the ones I would typically be on at that time of night, trying to score a late-night fix so my body's little fits wouldn't keep me up all night. An enjoyment that abruptly ended right about the time I almost ran over Lennie, who was trying to flag me down before I drove past the house where every light was off making it look deserted. Raising all kinds of questions for karma and the giggling voices in my head to taunt me with.

Using the sound of Lennie's screaming voice that he was yelling all kinds of obscenities at me with for guidance. I quickly backed up and pulled into the driveway of what I had hoped was still my home. Once in the driveway and out of the car, the voices that had been giggling with karma began asking all kinds of different questions about why the house looked so dark and deserted. Questions like, did Marie find out about my demotion that I was hoping to keep my little secret just a little longer? Or could it be because I was late and she figured that I slipped back into my old habits and decided just to cut ties with me while she could?

Still not sure if I was even welcome there, I slowly made my way down the stone walkway that was missing more than a couple of stones and passed the big bay window that showed no signs of anyone being there to the now very faded front door, hoping the whole time that my key would still turn the lock. With Lennie standing over my shoulder, bragging about the great stuff he got for our annual birthday smoke from this guy—who knows a guy—who gets it from this dude, I nervously placed my key in the deadbolt, turning it slowly all the way to the click of it unlocking like you might if you were defusing a bomb, allowing me to finally release the breath I had been holding the whole time. Wanting a little privacy just in case my worst fears were true and Marie decided to leave instead of me, I asked Lennie to take the box with my name on it that had ridden shotgun the whole white knuckle drive home and put it in the garage where I had planned to hide it so Marie wouldn't have to learn about my day's events unless she asked.

Seconds passed by like hours as I slowly opened the door just enough for me to slide my arm through to begin feeling around for the light switch so I could flip it to the "on" position, thinking the reason the house was so dark had nothing to do with the things the voices were still asking me about. But instead, the power company shut off the electric because of a missed payment that I was sure wasn't due for at least another day or two.

With the light switch in the "on" position, I was relieved to see the one or two lamps I hadn't sold light up the living room until I noticed Marie fast asleep on the recently purchased secondhand couch, clutching a pillow like she always did after going to bed mad, and the birthday part one of those different color letters "Happy Birthday" banners hanging on the stone fireplace mantle by little pieces of scotch tape while the

"Happy" part laid flat on the floor like it had been placed to tell the story that she was anything but.

Not wanting to disturb Marie in any way, I quietly made my way through the rest house, trying to figure out which one of the many things the voices were telling me could have had made Marie so upset. When I noticed a freshly smashed birthday cake on the same bar where I used to serve the boys their pan-sized pancakes and beside it, mixed in with those ads that no one reads, was a letter from the bank that held the deed to the only other thing that I hadn't sold, besides the lamps I just mentioned, that read "Notice of Auction" that was set to take place in just seven days from that moment, revealing karma's second move in the game I was unwillingly playing.

As I read the impossible request of the several thousands of dollars it would take to save the house Marie fell in love with twenty-some-odd years ago after reading the ad that seemed to be written just for us, the voices in my head that had been quietly giggling along with karma suddenly broke out laughing louder than they had ever laughed before, causing me to feel more than comfortable with a decision I would make in just a few hours from now.

Once I finished reading the letter that completely changed how I felt about the worst being behind me, I carefully placed it back in the stack of papers that was right next to the smashed birthday cake where I had found it and slowly made my way outside to the garage, where Lennie was busy preparing for our annual ritual of smoking marijuana while talking about what we hoped to accomplish in the upcoming year. For Lennie, it was the same as every year and that he was going to finally find a place of his own instead of his parents' nicely finished basement. As for me, it was to keep the house that meant so much to Marie that I had "less than enough time" to do it in.

After Lennie finished rolling the stuff that he had been bragging about since I almost ran him over a few minutes ago, he began looking through the box that I had planned on hiding from Marie, trying to find anything he could use to light the freshly rolled joint with while I sat quietly with the voices in my head and watched Lennie pulled out everything—from the pictures Marie had framed for my office wall to old pay stubs from when times were good and several of those plastic silverware napkin combos, leaving only a large folded-up legal-type document with "Monumental Life Insurance Company" written across the top in those fancy computer-generated script letters. Not sure where the insurance policy came from, let alone if it was mine, I began carefully reading every line, including where my name was actually written, along with a purchase date I don't remember and the amount I was worth after life was finished with me.

Now to say that the amount written on the policy would be enough to settle my debt with the bank before they invited a bunch of complete strangers to buy every memory Marie and I had made in the house for the lowest price possible would be an understatement—a seven-figure understatement to be exact. Not only was the amount enough to pay off the house, but there would be enough left over to replace everything I had sold, pawned, or traded, trying to keep up with the requests my body was continuously making for those once-prescribed pills just so I could function during the unforgiving hours required by my position at the dealership.

My dad once described life as nothing more than a bunch of "what the fuck moments" rolled up to fit neatly on a calendar until the day you die, and this was one of the moments. Here I was holding the answer to every financial problem that was going on in my life. The only problem was, for Marie to collect the enormous amount that was printed clearly on the top of the policy, I would have to take a permanent dirt nap, push up a few daisies, leave the world of the living or in simpler terms, be dead.

It wasn't my fear of death that was the problem; after all, I had already tried to end my life on three separate occasions—one of them successfully. Until another unfamiliar face, like the one who misled the friendly officer on the scene of my so-called accident that I was stable, shocked me back to life after I swallowed 145 pills that were supposed to help me deal with the anxiety of getting sober and life—in general, the first time I tried to end my relationship with the pills that were prescribed to me to help with the pain of getting hit by an SUV. No, the fear of dying wasn't the problem, but instead, a particular clause written in big bold letters, letting the reader know it's crucial they read it that said, "In the event of suicide, this policy becomes null and void no benefits paid," leaving Marie precisely like her older sister Sharon said I would, abandoned to clean up the mess I had made, and as much as I hate to say it, she would be right.

Over the next couple of hours or so, Lennie and I sat in the garage, breathing in the crisp September night air that just didn't seem to be as fresh as it was on my drive home and the smoke from the joint he finished rolling right before I found the life insurance policy that was going to save the house where Marie was still fast asleep on the secondhand couch. And as I sat in the last "less than sturdy" plastic chair Marie and I owned listening to Lennie talk about the good old days that had long since passed, I began thinking of all the ways I could hopefully make myself into nothing more than a sentimental something that gets talked about at special family gatherings without Marie, the insurance company, and of course, karma figuring out my death was no accident.

I quickly took the most commonly used ideas to cause one's own death off the list like bungee jumping without the cord, swallowing lead that's traveling at a high rate of speed, or accidentally cutting myself while shaving my wrists. Since I was fairly sure the insurance company would figure out that there was nothing accidental about any of them, maybe I could go to those areas where I used to buy my pills without a prescription, asking way too many questions and let the suspicions of who I may or may not be talking to take over. But I'm sure that my body would be hidden well enough to be listed as merely missing way past the upcoming sale, not solving any of the problems I was trying to solve. Natural causes weren't at all a possibility even with all the cigarettes I have been chain-smoking, along with the liver damage that must have occurred with all the pills I had swallowed over the past three years. Since I knew that if karma had anything to do with it, I would live long past the sound of the gavel falling followed by the words "Sold to the lovely couple in the back," giving me more life than I wanted to look at the disappointment in the crystal-blue eyes of the one that means more to me than my last breath.

As a last resort, I could maybe convince any officer that I was holding something that was more dangerous than the plastic version I actually had in my hand. Committing the proverbial "suicide by cop," but I couldn't see burdening anyone with my problems just for doing their job. Not to mention, I don't think I even had the ninety-nine cents it would take to buy that something since my last ten bucks went as a deposit on Mr. Jackson's car in a weak attempt to make something good come out of the day.

After several more "puff-puff-pass" moments with Lennie, and "that would do the trick ideas" I was thinking about in the privacy of my head. I snubbed out the "little less than half" a joint we had been smoking. Ending our annual birthday ritual that we had been doing for the past twenty-plus years, and began loading all the pictures Marie framed for me of times I don't remember, pay stubs from when times were good, and those plastic silverware napkin combos I can't seem to get away from, back into the box with my last name scribbled on it that I had planned on hiding from Marie—everything, except for the piece of paper that was worth more than enough to settle my debt with the bank before the upcoming sale of the house my sons grew up in, leaving only the question of how I would say goodbye to those stupid always-constant sunrises my brother made such a big deal about at the beginning of my unconventional rehab, finally quieting the voices in my head that seemed to be working hand in hand with karma.

Chapter 7

Ticket Please

"SUICIDE" IS DEFINED as an impulsive act, causing one's own death due to stress from such things as financial difficulties, troubles with relationships, and so on. The "Good Book" that people go to learn about every Sunday, Christmas, and Easter, while trying to impersonate the decent person that's described in its pages that usually only lasts until they exit the church, says that suicide is a sin. That life is a precious gift from above, "not to be taken for granted" even though it's sometimes like that ugly sweater Grandma gets you that spends the rest of its time hidden in the deepest part of your closet so no one will ever see it.

Others will say suicide is just a selfish way out of some of life's more complicated situations. Those are the same people that have never been trapped inside their own head, where the only thing that gives comfort is forfeiting whatever is left of your very existence. As for me, well, I think it's just the different outlook that you have on that so-called overrated "precious gift" called life when you realize that you are more of a liability to everyone that's ever mattered to you.

With everything packed neatly in the box that I should have hidden from Marie already. Lennie and I sat for I'm really not sure how long, watching the rainfall through the open garage door talking about things that would probably only make any sense if you smoked what we just smoked. When Lennie reached in his pocket and pulled out a bag of his mom's special peanut butter cookie crumbs, a staple meal after all our puff, puff, pass session and what I hoped was a couple of dollars for gas like we discussed when I first agreed to take him home just a day or so ago. That turned out to be what looked like a birthday present wrapped in my favorite comic book hero, Batman, wrapping paper, that had, "To me, from Lennie" written on it, in his mother's handwriting. Confirming my suspicion that she was the one that actually did the wrapping.

A little surprised over the birthday gift Lennie's mom wrapped for me since gift giving wasn't something we did, I gave Lennie the usual "You shouldn't have," then began opening the perfectly wrapped gift, that revealed a picture of a much younger both of us standing together someplace I don't remember and inscribed on the frame was two words that almost convinced me to change my plans about how I was going to save the house that Marie loved so much that read, "Best Friends," leaving for only the second time, my gift of gab, quiet.

There is an unwritten rule among males that you never show any type of emotion, a rule I quickly broke the moment my eyes started to water up over the most thoughtful "anything" Lennie had ever done or given me since we first met at that fast food place that sold roast beef sandwiches and mocha shakes so many years ago, blaming it entirely on the cloud of smoke that was still lingering over our heads, of course. Still too choked up to speak over the unexpected gift Lennie's mother wrapped, I carefully placed the picture on top of the box that held all my other perfectly framed "never around" memories of days that I could never get back no matter how hard I tried and gave Lennie what you might call a "love you like a brother" hug, giving him my best "thank you" possible without having to say a single word.

At just a minute or two past my birthday, the rain that Lennie and I had been watching through the open garage suddenly stopped. So we decided it's time to take the short ride to Lennie's bachelor pad located at his parents' house, accidentally leaving the box I had planned to hide from Marie that told the story of how my day went in plain sight between the two "less than sturdy" plastic chairs Lennie and I had been sitting on during our annual birthday smoke with the picture of a much younger both of us, sitting on top of it for anyone who entered the garage to see.

Once Lennie and I were both "buckled up for safety" in the car that the well-known secret Matt picked for me to use as a demo, I turned the ignition to the start position, making sure I was still just "almost" out of gas before backing out of the driveway, marked by several shrubs on one side and tall pine trees on the other, stopping halfway to stare at the darkened house that I was going to save with the piece of paper that was now safely in my back pocket and the stupid "precious little gift" called life that I was becoming more and more determined to return.

During the just over so many miles ride to Lennie's bachelor pad in his parents' basement, I began discussing with the voices in my head about what my next move should be in the game karma just didn't seem to want to end while listening to Lennie do his worst karaoke to a song about being at the "End of the Line" that was playing on the radio and the wind blowing in my ear from the "slightly rolled down" window I was using as an ashtray for the last few cigarettes I had left, deciding that tomorrow would be best for everyone else I cared about without me changing the rules to the game without karma knowing.

After a couple more of Lennie's worst karaoke sessions to whatever song was playing on the radio that I eventually did backup vocals too, we slowly pulled into his parents' driveway, making sure to lower the volume of the radio and turn off the headlights like we did every time I was Lennie's ride home so his parents wouldn't know how far past curfew he was since their room was right at the front of the house. Confident his parents were sound asleep since we didn't see any of the lights in their room suddenly turn on or hear his dad yell out the window, "Who the hell is here at this hour? Some people have to work in the morning you know!" Lennie asked me to give him a few minutes so he could run inside to get the gas money he promised from his mom's purse, hopefully without waking her since she probably didn't know anything about loaning it to him.

Knowing that Lennie wasn't what you might call graceful, I wasn't at all surprised to hear the sound of something breaking after a few minutes of watching the bright light from the cell phone he was using for a flashlight, moving sporadically through the dark house, causing the light in his parents' bedroom to come on and Lennie to yell, "Don't worry, it's just me getting something to drink!" before his dad could ask the question of "Who was there at this hour?" while Lennie continued his search of the still dark house for his mom's purse where the gas money he promised me was. I sat quietly outside in the car, talking with the voices in my head about all the responsible adult stuff I needed to do before I ended my overstayed welcome on this side of life, things like my last will and testament even though all my most valuable assets were already in the hands of the pawnshop, Facebook buy, sell, trade customers, and the dealers I had gotten to know over the several years that would let me use property as trade instead of the usual cash for those pills that my body was continually requiring just to function in my everyday life. A few minutes passed before Lennie finally made his way through the less-than-quiet screen door and down the rain-covered driveway to the car, where I had been discussing all my final arrangements with the voices in my head and handed me the only cash he could find that was in the form of a five-dollar winning lottery ticket since he only had a few seconds to look after breaking the very sentimental vase that had made the loud crashing sound I heard, waking his parents up long enough for them to be "okay" with the so-called "I'm thirsty" lie Lennie told to cover up what he was really doing.

A little frustrated, I thanked Lennie for the what he called "better than cash" lotto ticket he gave me for gas and the picture of us together from more than a couple of years ago that meant more to me than he could ever imagine before telling him "goodbye" instead of the usual "See you later" we always said to each other when we parted ways, just in case I was successful on my goal to save what "little bit of nothing" that I had left in this miserable world I had created for myself before I would see my best friend again. Changing the typical smirk, he used as his everyday smile to more of a concerned look. Causing him to tell me something I already knew—that no matter what was going on, good, bad, or indifferent, he would always have my back.

With what I was hoping to be my final goodbye to Lennie said I lit up one of the "less than three" cigarettes I had in my last pack while he made his way back inside the bachelor pad he always bragged about, screaming one last time "It's just me" to the light that had turned back on from the room in the front of the house after I started the car, and headed to the closest anything that would take Lennie's mom lottery ticket for the gas I was sure I would need to make it home even though it didn't look like the gas hand had moved at all from the just over the capital "E" position it was in after taking Lennie home as promised just the day before.

It would take about twenty-five streetlights, twice as many potholes, and the song on the radio about "Old-Time Rock and Roll" Marie always did her best impersonation of a famous movie scene to when she thought I wasn't watching, complete with shades, hairbrush microphone, and one of my button-up shirts she liked to use as pajamas that I was playing louder than the recommended volume to end before I pulled into the closest somewhere that sold gas and most importantly lottery tickets like one I planned on paying for my much-needed gas with.

Happy I made it to safely in front of pump one without the car, I just knew the well-known secret Matt picked for me to use out of spite, running out of gas, I placed the winning lottery ticket in the pocket of the jacket Marie bought for me the day we spent shopping at every secondhand store to replace the clothes that I had grown too small to fit in, protecting it from the rain that had begun to fall and went inside the place where karma would test the validity of my sanity for the insane plans I was still trying figuring out with the voices in my head.

Still conversing with the voices about how my up-and-coming demise would happen, I opened the door to the place that sold gas and lottery tickets, setting off a little chime that let the nice man behind the counter, and what looked like bulletproof glass know that he had another customer other than the overly enthusiastic young couple, who were buying every "I don't have a clue about relationship" gifts. Including a stuffed bear for her, some sunglasses for him, and a vintage "earlier that week" bottle of wine that had a big round orange sticker on it, that read "Special" for both of them to share.

Once inside and out of the chilly rain that started falling seconds before my arrival, I stood by the door for a minute or so, calculating in my head to see if there were enough winnings from the five-dollar lottery ticket to not only get enough gas for the rest of the ride home but something cold to drink to help with the dry mouth that comes with smoking the illegal tobacco Lennie got from this guy—who knows a guy—who gets it from this dude just a couple of hours before. Felling safe that I did the math right in my head, I made my way past the overly enthusiastic young couple, who were now using the words "I love you," like there was a shortage, and headed to the back where the coolers were to grab the cheapest cold anything to drink before going to the front to pay it and three-dollar worth of gas on pump one.

Impressed on how I was able to make it past all the chips, cookies, and cakes that were piquing my interest because of the munchies I was experiencing, I casually told the nice man in the bulletproof fortress behind the counter that I need three dollars on pump one then placed the winning lottery ticket, along with the cold whatever I had gotten from the store's cooler in the drawer that the nice man pushed out for me and waited for him to cash the ticket that I was expecting a little change back from, but instead, all I got was the "wait for it" part of the joke karma always like to tell.

I watched as the nice man behind the glass scan the ticket not once, not twice, but three times before letting me know that it was no good and that he would need cash or a credit card to complete the less-than-five-dollar purchase—none of which I had, of course, since I used my last ten dollars on Mr. Jackson's recent purchase. With my composure barely in check, I asked to see the ticket since I was sure that the three matching treasure chests required for it to be a winner were clearly visible then slid the ticket back through the bank-style drawer and demanded him complete my just-a-little-over-four-dollar purchase so I could go home. After finishing whatever it was he was doing on his phone, the now-not-so-friendly guy behind the bulletproof glass looked at me and said, "The ticket expired at midnight, and since it's now ten minutes past midnight, you needed to pay with the cash or a credit card like he mentioned before or leave" because he had other customers like the more-than-affectionate couple who now laughing along with the voices in my head over karmas well-planned move.

Embarrassed, humiliated, and just plain mad, I pushed by the now laughing couple who was waiting to pay for those pointless romantic gifts that would one day be nothing more than another long-forgotten something in a trash can somewhere, and out the door to the car that I was sure the idiot who had his feet on my desk earlier that day picked for me, knowing damn well that the tank was as empty as my wallet, and headed home to the place that would soon belong to someone else if I did not complete my plans to cash in the piece of paper that was still in my back pocket.

After I pulled away from pump "One," that I didn't get a single drop of gas from, and out of the parking lot that was suddenly full of people that may or may not, have actually been there laughing. Karma finally decided to give me the first clue to her intent that came in the form of a bright amber light that spelled out the words "Low Fuel," quickly followed by the spitting and sputtering of the car's motor because of an empty tank of gas that would eventually lead to the always-on-time 2:00 a.m. freight train.

Chapter 8

All Aboard

IRONY IS SOMETIMES defined as a state of affairs or events that seem to be deliberate contrary to what one thinks, often ending in an amusing result, or punch line if you will. And even though I was far from laughing, sitting on the side of the road in a car that was refusing to go any further because of lack of gas, I could understand why karma might find it funny since it was me who was the punch line of the ironic joke she was telling and not her.

Still not quite sure why karma had taken such a special interest in my personal misery—after all, I hadn't used any kind of anything since the day—I decided to call my older brother for some of his unconventional rehab. I sat quietly on the side of the road in the car that was refusing to start because of the lack of gas, listening to the "more than several" passer byers that we're laughing in perfect harmony with the voices in my head, I was sure no one else heard. Trying to gather what little bit of rational thinking I had left so I could finally figure out the perfect way to complete the irrational plans I was making, in the privacy of my mind, to forfeit this game between karma and me, so all those that I cared so much about could move on with their life without the extra weight of a washed-up addict like me holding them back. When I heard the sound of the 1:30 a.m. train getting ready to cross the road I was on that I knew would be followed in precisely thirty minutes by the always-on-time 2:00 a.m. one that would be perfect for my accidental not at well-planned death.

With several words of encouragement from the voices in my head that seemed to think my idea would work, I stepped out of the car that was refusing to start and began calculating the distance between me and the tracks, where I was planning to catch the 2:00 a.m. train at, car and all, that was only about a hundred feet away and at the bottom of a hill, making the physical part of getting the car where I needed it to be in the next "less than twenty-five minutes" not at all a problem since all I had to do was put the car in neutral and let gravity do the rest, leaving only the mental strength that I was beginning to lose the hardest part of the plan.

It wasn't the fear of death that was putting a strain on my mental stability because, like I told you, in the beginning, I had already become more than comfortable with not having any more of those overrated consistent sunrises that my older brother foolishly bragged about while drinking his way to strong coffee the first day of my unconventional rehab. Instead, it was more of all the moments that had long passed that I took for granted in a failed attempt to build my pride over the whole lot of nothing I had accomplished to prove those who didn't matter at all anymore wrong when they said I wouldn't, but as the saying goes, "Pride is a poor substitute for intelligence," leaving me the dumbest suicide statistic in history.

Prepared to put my plan into action, I took a quick look around the quiet street to make sure that none of the passersby, who was laughing along with the voices in my head, instead of offering me a helping hand, were watching then took a seat behind the steering wheel, leaving the driver's door open so I could hear the sound of the train's horn, signaling that it was close to the street I was on and lit one of the last three cigarettes I had left with an old brass lighter Marie and the boys gave me for my twenty-first birthday when I thought for sure I knew what my future was going to be. None of which included me standing on the top of a hill just a hundred feet and slightly under seventeen minutes away from my final goodbye to this side of the life, listening to the sound of crickets chirping among themselves in the night and the continuous humming sound of the streetlights that were lighting the way like a runway at any airport.

While waiting for the always-on-time 2:00 a.m. train to give me a lift to the other side of life, I finished the last of three cigarettes I had left before quickly lighting one of the two left in the pack my youngest son, Austin, bought me as a birthday present then looked up to the dark but clear sky above to ask whoever it was that was supposed to be up there for the strength to do what I needed to do even though I was pretty sure that the whoever might be up there was probably laughing just as hard as the overly enthusiastic young couple that bought that cheap bottle of wine with the big orange sticker on it that read "Special" and the passerby who seemed to vanish seconds after I made up my mind to finally end the pain of being me and the game with karma that I never wanted to play.

Without a single response from the whoever may or may not be above and more than enough words from those voices in my head that sounded like they were now, making bets with karma on whether or not I had the nerve to do what I have been talking about doing since running out of gas just one hundred feet and minutes away from the train I have been patiently waiting for, I took a deep breath of the fresh air that was blowing, which smelled just like the little bit of perfume Marie was wearing, along with the sexiest red dress I have ever seen her in the night I came home late for our twentieth anniversary because Mr. and Mrs. Richardson needed a van for the family vacation they were taking a week from that day. I then placed the leg I planned on using for leverage on the still-wet ground and the car in neutral, making sure to leave the other foot on the brake so I wouldn't accidentally get a head start, missing the opportunity to cash in the seven-figure policy that was in my back pocket where I was sure the person that pronounced me DOA or dead on arrival would find it, giving Marie more than enough money to pay the bank before they invited anyone and everyone with a checkbook or perfect credit rating to buy the house she loved so much.

Completely skipping any kind of a countdown, like the ones NASA gives all the astronauts that are buckled up for safety in the space shuttle before taking off to maybe meet the someone who never responded to my request for strength, the train I had been waiting for suddenly blurted out its first warning to let anyone that might be on the tracks know it's time to quickly move since there would be a slim-to-none chance of it stopping in time to prevent the reasonably well-planned "accident" I was beginning to get a little excited about, causing me to take one foot off the brake and use the other one that was resting nervously on the damp street to push starting the car, which belonged to the dealership, to begin rolling directly in front of the always-on time 2:00 a.m. train.

It didn't take much effort from the foot resting on the damp street to get the car rolling in the right direction, and as the streetlights started to pass by a little faster, some of the good memories karma was keeping under lock and key somehow slipped past her watchful eye and began playing like an old movie that was written just for me. Memories like how soft Marie's lips were the first time I kissed her at the falls, where we had our first date that consisted of conversation, cold fried chicken, and something else, I seem to have forgotten about, followed by several of Marie and our two sons, playing in the backyard on the now-abandoned swing set that was right next to the big oak tree where I first agreed to buy the house she loved so much without even really knowing the price. But the one that stood out the most was the day Marie said the words "I, Marie, take you to be my lawfully wedded husband to have and to hold, from this day forward, for better or worse, for richer or poorer, in sickness and in health until death do us part..." that was about to take place at any time now.

Now safely in the perfect position for the always-on-time 2:00 a.m. train to be part of the accident where I was hoping to lose my life and the movie of the few good memories that slipped past karma's watchful eye over, I gripped the steering wheel in the perfect ten and two positions, took a deep breath, and began watching as the light from the oncoming train got closer and closer, lighting the inside of the car before closing my eyes so I wouldn't have to know what was going to happen to any of the pieces of me that might be left after the impact and screamed as loud as I could, "I love you, pickles," hoping the wind that was still blowing would carry those words through one of the windows Marie liked to keep during these chilly fall night, giving her some kind of comfort after my recent passing.

After noticing that the ground wasn't shaking nearly as bad as before and the sound of the train's warning signal getting further and further away from the spot where I parked the car that the well-known secret Matt picked for me to use as a demo, I opened my eyes just in time to catch a glimpse of the last car belonging to the always-on-time 2:00 a.m. cargo train, passing directly behind where I was parked, letting me know that I was right back where I spent most of my addiction—on the wrong side of the tracks. Now most people would take this as some kind of divine intervention everyone could talk about while passing around the collection plate at church on Sunday. As for me, I took it personally, and just like Helen did over the "no pickle" on her hamburger request, that only she heard, I demanded to speak to the manager. Mad as hell, I pushed open the driver's side door of the car that I was hoping would be in more pieces than it was and began screaming several choice words to whoever it was interfering with my plans to save the house Marie loved so much, letting them know that they had no idea who they were dealing with in an attempt to make myself sound a little more important than I actually was. When karma suddenly responded with the unexpected 2:15 a.m. train that arrived on the same track where the car, that I was now financially responsible for, was parked, letting me know that she wasn't a fan of idle threats and that I had no idea who I was dealing with.

A little disoriented from karma's response to the few choice words and idle threats I was yelling in her direction, I watched as every dark house I coasted by just minutes before started to light up one porch at a time while patting myself down like I was looking for something in the pockets of the secondhand clothes I was wearing, hoping to find some kind of terminal wound so I wouldn't have to explain to anyone why the car I was driving was on fire in front of the unexpected 2:15 a.m. train, only to find a small burn hole from the cigarette that feel out of my mouth after realizing that I missed my opportunity to be the fatality the news would talk about during their "live on the scene" report and a small red spot that turned out to be a jelly stain from the doughnut I took from the service department waiting room earlier the day before instead of blood like I was hoping for.

Someone must have taken a few minutes to call the police about the recent disturbance my poorly planned accident caused before joining everyone else that was now standing outside in their "whatever they wore to bed" clothes, sipping coffee, trying to figure out the who, what, and why part of the accident that I would answer with the lie I was now rehearsing with the voices in my head.

Because I soon started to see the flashing red-and-blue lights that were on top of the same car, that the same friendly officer was driving earlier the day before when he let me off with a warning for going a little faster than the posted speed limit because it was my birthday, slowly maneuvering through the debris that was now covering the road so he could figure out who it was that had foolishly parked on the wrong track, causing the collision with the wrong train that turned out to be me and an unnamed coconspirator who, I was sure, was laughing at the perfectly executed move she had made in the game that I was now not only fully prepared to play but was even more determined to win.

Chapter 9

The Sunny Side of Scrambled

"HOW ARE YOU doing today?" is a question that you often hear in the checkout line of any retail store as a way of making you feel like they care about you that usually only lasts until you get the receipt completing the purchase of something you don't need or can afford. And that's precisely the way the friendly officer, who arrived on the scene of my recent poorly planned accident, driving one of those fancy cars with the red-and-blue lights on the top, started our conversation together as if the pile of smashed and burning car wasn't a clue that my day might not be going as well as you might think.

With a completely different outlook on my chances of winning the game karma should have never invited me to play, I sat quietly on the curb, smoking my very last cigarette, watching as the friendly officer, who, after giving his name, followed by some numbers and the words, "On scene, send fire and rescue" to the little microphone on his shoulder and began questioning the group of spectators that were still drinking coffee and now pointing in my direction about what caused all the early morning excitement before walking over to where I was sitting for my version of the events that would be anything but the truth.

Now the center of attention and the prime suspect in the mess I created, with a little help from karma, of course, I spent the next what seemed like forever, repeating the far-from-a-true story that I was making up as I went along to the friendly officer and anyone else within ear distance of our conversation that couldn't be bothered just a few minutes before when I ran out of gas about one hundred feet from where I was being questioned, making sure to leave out the part where I was the one who gave the car the push it needed to get to the wrong set tracks just in time for the unexpected 2:15 a.m. train karma must have been driving, to hit it, barely escaping with a life that I didn't want anymore.

After giving the friendly officer my version of events that didn't really happen and the now-no-longer-concerned citizens, who had been trying to convince me of how lucky I was to be alive, headed back to their cozy lives inside the four walls of their homes to get ready for the new day that had arrived, I stood up, dusted myself off, and prepared to start the just under a half-mile walk to my "soon-to-be previous residence" when I noticed a silver truck with the words "Custom-Built Furniture" on the side and a phone number I recognized that belonged to the only person that was able to quiet the voices in my head— my older brother.

Having no reason to be in my part of town that early in the morning, I just assumed Marie must have been a little worried about me since we hadn't seen or spoken to each other since she dropped me off in front of the side door of the dealership the previous day after telling me the lie about being sexy and decided it was best to call my brother to complete the task she asked me to do the day she finally drew her line in the sand over my addiction that was written in a note of so few words but said so much, "Find the man she had fallen in love with so long ago" that I was pretty sure was gone forever.

Knowing that my older brother would in no way believe the anything-but-true story I told the friendly officer, EMTs, and the spectators that were now nowhere to be found, I began rehearsing a little more truthful version of that morning events in my head as I watched him casually step out of the "not at all new" truck I had sold him when I first started at the dealership more than a couple of years ago and begin looking around at the mess I made in my attempt to cash in the policy insurance policy that was in the same pocket as the new eighty-five-dollar ticket for "failure to control" the friendly officer gave me after the EMTs on the scene were done checking all my vitals that I was certain were fine, ending the continuous battle that was going on inside my head between me, the voices, and of course, karma that was consuming my every rational thought.

After looking around for a minute or two, while shaking his head the same way our dad did after we may or may not have done something foolish, my older brother adjusted the old hat he always wore, brushed the sawdust off his pants that always seemed to be there, and lit a cigarette from the pack in his shirt pocket before walking over to where the friendly officer was still writing down the "far from accurate" story I had told him a few minutes before. I'm not sure what my brother told the friendly officer that seemed to make him laugh a little before signaling me that I was free to go. It could have been the whole lawn mower story from the week or so ago when I first reunited with Marie after my unconventional rehab, or maybe it was that something our dad told him in the privacy of just the two of them after one of our parents' regular disputes over who was best to raise us. Either way, I was happy that I wouldn't have to explain to Marie why I was in the local jail needing bail money I was sure we didn't have, only where I had been all night that would be a lie I promised never to tell again.

With the "okay" to leave from the friendly officer, I quickly walked over to my older brother's truck in case some mind changing took place after everyone on the scene figured out my story was complete bullshit then carefully opened the passenger door so none of the several coffee cups that were missing from the kitchen sink full of "wash when needed" dishes at his place would fall out and sat inside impatiently, watching through the sawdust and nicotine-stained windshield of the old truck as my brother finished thanking everyone that was still on the scene of my so-called accidental run-in with the unexpected 2:15 a.m. train for helping his little brother who, as he explained, was just having one of those kinds of days.

After thanking everyone, from the friendly officer to the guy still sweeping up parts from the car I parked on the wrong track at the right time, my brother climbed into the driver's seat of the still running old truck, put it in gear, and began heading in the opposite direction of the house that would be sold to the "lovely couple in the back" if I didn't cash in the insurance policy that was in the same pocket as my new eighty-five-dollar failure to control ticket I could in no way pay. Causing me to wonder if Marie took my not coming home all night as I was back to my old habits from just over a month ago and requested my brother take me anywhere but there.

Convinced I wasn't welcome back at the house I intended to give my last breath to save and my miscalculated accident in the rearview mirror of the old truck where I hoped to keep it, I sat quietly, staring out the passenger window, watching all the people who may or may not have been there, refusing to stop laughing with the voices in my head long enough for me to plan my next hopefully fatal accident when my older brother suddenly pulled into the parking lot of a local fast-food restaurant and called who, I could only assume, was Marie to let her know that she could call off the search for the fool in the passenger seat and that after we got a little something to eat, he would bring me to where the best part of me was waiting. I have to admit, I was more than a little bit surprised that Marie hadn't called it quits on our twenty-some-odd years of marriage after I never made it home from dropping Lennie off at his bachelor pad located in his parents' basement and that there was no mention of the box I was sure she found exactly where I left it for anyone who entered the garage to see.

In an attempt to hide the little bit of hope I was feeling from karma after listening to one side of the phone conversation between my brother and who, I could only assume, was Marie, I continued staring out the passenger side window, at all the people in the parking lot, who seemed to be unaware of my screams to whoever it was in the sky that was supposed to answer my request for death while my brother pulled into the drive-through lane of the fast-food restaurant and up to the menu for the "little something to eat" part of the conversation I just overheard.

After a few minutes of no one in the truck saying a word about the phone conversation my brother just had with who, I wasn't sure, was Marie, the sound of a young lady's voice came over the far-from-functioning speaker attached to the menu, welcoming us to whatever the name of the restaurant was followed by "would you like to try some kind of new menu item" that my brother quickly declined before ordering two of the largest, strongest cups of coffee they had to offer, one large diet of whatever they had, and a bag full of strawberry biscuits that were actually just several plain biscuits with as many packs of strawberry jelly the restaurant is willing to give after pleading like a five-year-old wanting something his mom just said they couldn't have. With a little chuckle in her voice over the way, my brother pleaded like someone a lot younger than his actual age for extra packets of jelly. The young lady, who I hadn't seen yet, read back the unusual order before giving the total and directions to the next window where everything would be waiting after he paid.

Realizing my brother ordered the same kind of breakfast our dad would order when he was about to have a heart-to-heart conversation about some of the lies our pretend to be mother may have said about him, I decided to put the plans I was making in the privacy of my head on hold so I could come up with a more believable story about what I was really doing that morning since I was positive my brother wouldn't believe a word of the one I told everyone at the scene of my first failed attempt to erase tomorrow off my to-do list.

Once in front of the window the young lady gave us directions to, my brother reached in his pocket and pulled out several clumped-up dollar bills to pay for the breakfast I was sure he was going to use as the ice breaker for a conversation I didn't want to have then handed me one of the coffees, placing the other beside the large diet whatever they had in a cupholder located just below a picture of his two kids that he gets to see from time to time when his ex-wife needs something and the bag of strawberry biscuits in the seat between us. With the exchange of cash for a "little something to eat" complete, my brother thanked the young lady, who seemed to enjoy his Southern accent, for all the extra strawberry jelly that had to be put in a bag all its own before pulling the old truck into an out-of-the-way parking space behind the restaurant so we could hopefully eat without having the conversation I was in no mood to have.

I managed to get a couple of sips of the large strong coffee my body was begging for since I hadn't slept since the guy on the radio lied to me about "what a beautiful day it was going to be" before my brother broke the awkward silence I was happy with by telling me something that wouldn't make sense to me for at least a couple more days or so. "I don't know what bullshit story you told the friendly officer. That's your lie. I'm sure you told it like you had to, but don't try it with me because I know better. Now before you go making any more irrational plans like the one this morning, remember this, no matter how scrambled your life may be right now, there is a sunny side if you can just remember these three things. First, life's not all that complicated. It's people that make it that way. Second, the submissive one is always in control, and finally, remember this, Marie doesn't need you! And once you figure that out, you will realize that you are one of the few that has kissed the most beautiful girl in the world."

After my brother finished his speech and the large diet of whatever the restaurant had on hand and possibly his third strawberry biscuit, he reached in his shirt pocket and handed me a cigarette to enjoy with what was left of the large strong coffee I had been nursing while trying not to make eye contact with all the people that couldn't hear my screams just minutes earlier, who seemed to disappear just like everyone at the gas station that was laughing over my couple-of-minute expired lottery ticket Lennie gave me for gas money that would eventually leave me on the wrong track at the right time before putting the old truck in gear and heading to the house Marie loved so much that would only take my last breath to save.

During what seemed to take forever ride back to where I wasn't sure Marie would be waiting, no one in the old truck said a word except for the idiot on the radio who was telling the same lie he told the day before and, of course, the voices in my head who, under karma's direction, began reminding me of all the explaining I would have to do about where I had been all night and the box I had no doubt Marie already found that in no way could be truthful, causing the hopeful feeling I was sure I hid from karma to quickly change into determination, especially after we made the right onto Helena Avenue, where I noticed something other than the far-from-new clunker Marie had gotten during my unconventional rehab in the driveway of my soon-to-be-previous residence.

Chapter 10

To Be Determined

DETERMINED IS A word often used to describe someone that has overcame life's little adversities, creating what is considered a perfect life by those who work in the marketing department of every major corporation, where everyone we care about is happy, and the sun always shines unless they are selling cold medicine, four-wheel drives vehicles, or a new kind of travel mug said to keep your coffee warmer longer than every other one you have tried. And even though I knew all you need in life is, food, water, and shelter, two of which at one time I didn't have, I was more determined to give Marie the same kind of life those guys created in all the TV commercials everything except for the always sunny part; after all, I don't have any control over the weather.

With the ride to the house, I was sure somebody would get for less than the fair market price at the upcoming bank auction if I failed to cancel all my plans for living past today, taking a lot longer than I expected and the coffee I had been nursing since we left the restaurant all but gone. I decided to make my appearance look better than it did, by brushing what little hair I had left and any dirt or jelly that was on the secondhand clothes I had been wearing since the day before. As we got closer to where I didn't know what was going to happen, I tried to block out the voices' taunts and snickers by sneaking another peek at those memories karma didn't like me to see. Memories like the long walks Marie and I would take around the neighborhood because she was worried I was getting a little soft in the middle after too many years sitting behind a desk or how beautiful her smile was when it would appear just above the coffee mug she was drinking from while drawing a heart on the glass in the big bay window you walked past on the way to the in need of paint front door as her way of saying "I love you" without speaking a single word.

It wasn't until just after my brother made the last right onto Helena Avenue where the boys would wait to catch the bus to school and passed the Jones's house where I couldn't help but noticed both of them standing in the front yard, having what you might call a less-than-friendly discussion over something I had no clue or cared about, that I first noticed a car I didn't recognize sitting in the driveway right behind our new family clunker and a strange man I didn't know standing at the old brown door telling Marie something that seemed to make her smile the same way I haven't in a long time.

In an effort to hide the unorganized chaos that was going on in my head after seeing what I figured was my replacement, I quickly asked my brother to drive around the block one last time, telling him the strange car driven by someone I didn't know was probably just another bill collector that I was in no mood to argue with over some payment I couldn't make even though I was sure Marie had moved on to someone better than I ever was and me not coming home all night was all she needed to finally call it quits on our twenty-some-odd years of marriage.

It didn't take nearly as long as I would've liked for my brother to make the four left turns around the block and into the driveway where the car I didn't recognize was parked just a minute or two ago. My brother must have overheard the voices telling me what Marie might be doing with the guy who seemed to make her smile the same way she did when we first met the summer before my senior of high school because after taking the last sip from the large diet part of the bag full of strawberry biscuit breakfast, that was still sitting in the seat between us, my brother looked over at me with the same grin I had seen many times during my unconventional rehab and said, "Oh, the pictures our minds can paint when we assume," chuckling as if I wasn't thinking exactly what my brother already knew I was. I jumped out of the passenger side of the truck, but not before grabbing one of his fresh packs of cigarettes from behind the bag of strawberry biscuits and telling the only person the seemed to be able to quiet the voices, "See you when I see you," causing the smirk he always wore to quickly disappear as if he knew that the breakfast and fresh pack of smokes didn't change any of my plans to check out of life early.

As I watched my brother pull out of the driveway, blaring a song about being "Eastbound and Down" like our dad did every time it came on the radio, I asked the voices in my head to give me just a few minutes of privacy so I could prepare the lie I didn't want to tell Marie about what happened that kept me out all night and began making my way to the same door where the guy that seemed to make her smile like I haven't in some time was standing just a few minutes before, careful not to make eye contact with my reflection in the big bay window since I still couldn't stand the sight of me.

Expecting to find the old brown door locked and a second note from Marie explaining why I wasn't welcome there anymore attached to the green bag I never unpacked, I was more than a little surprised to see Marie standing there with her arms crossed and foot tapping like she would do when questioning the boys about which one of them did something that she specifically told them not to do.

Not having all the details to the far-from-truthful story I was planning to tell Marie worked out in my head, I cautiously took two long steps around her and into the house, making sure to stay out of range of her signature punch to the arm, like the one she always gave me after I forget something important like our twentieth wedding anniversary. Once I was semisafe inside the house I still wasn't sure I was welcome at, Marie slammed the old brown door closed behind me so the neighbors wouldn't hear her screaming all the who, what, when questions about why I never came home after work the day before that I could in no way answer truthfully. Marie was about two minutes into her rant about who I thought I was to make her worry the way she did and how lucky I was that my brother found me before she did when I noticed the anger in her crystal-blue eyes suddenly turn to concern over the red stain on the secondhand shirt she picked out for me the night before my return to the dealership, allowing me to begin telling her the not-completely-true story I repeated over and over to everyone at the scene of my so-called accidental run-in with the unexpected 2:15 a.m. that karma knew was coming, making sure to leave out the parts where I found the letter about the upcoming sale of the house she loved so much and the strange someone I saw her talking to the first time I passed the house that I was sure she was getting ready to replace me with.

After I finished the mostly made-up story about all my adventures from the night before, Marie slowly made her way to the secondhand couch that replaced the fancy one I sold to the lovely couple from one of those Facebook buy sell groups to feed my addiction, sat down, looked at me with the same look she had when she first heard about the passing of her parents and began asking the standard, "Are you okay?" and "Is that red stain on your shirt blood?" questions, trying not to make eye contact with her crystal-blue eyes, fearing she might see through all the lies I just told her, breaking a promise I made the day I came home from ending my three-year relationship with those little pills my body still requests from time to time. I reassured Marie that I was fine and that the red stain was just some strawberry jelly from the biscuits me and my brother had for breakfast. After a few more minutes of "I'm sorry for yelling the way I did" and "I'm just happy you're okay," Marie excused herself so she could take what she called a calm down shower, leaving me just enough time to check the status of the box that had my name and the word "junk" written on it I just knew Marie found exactly where I left it the now night before.

Once Marie was halfway up the stairs and me out of her line of sight, I headed out the large sliding doors to the garage, where I left the box sitting between the two less-than-comfortable plastic chairs Lennie and I were using during our annual birthday smoke session. It wasn't until I was standing by the large oak tree where I agreed to buy the house without even really knowing the price that I first noticed the garage door Lennie and I were watching the rainfall through was closed unlike how I left it when I took Lennie home, raising the question of how much of my far-from-a-truthful story about what kept me out all night did Marie already know was a lie. Hoping Marie closed the overhead garage door without paying any attention to what was sitting in plain sight, I carefully pushed open the small door that we haven't kept lock since I sold everything of value to Jim's Pawnshop during my pill-chasing days and cautiously looked inside only to find the box I was so worried about missing from the spot where I left it, thinking that even if Marie found the box that told the truth about what happened the day before, there was a slim-to-none chance that she never looked inside and that I had better continue the search.

After several minutes of looking for the box that was nowhere to be found, I heard Marie calling me to join her on the patio where she would watch the boys play on the now-abandoned swing set for a cup of coffee before I left for my second day back at the dealership. In order to buy a little more time for my search, I told Marie to give me a few minutes, and I'll be right there. Something she must not have heard because by the time I could finish my sentence, there she was standing in the doorway of the garage holding two cups of coffee, wearing nothing but a towel on her head like she always wore after a shower and one of my shirts that she always liked to borrow, leaving me more than breathless. Knowing that she now had my undivided attention, Marie handed me one of the cups of coffee she was holding before whispering in my ear, "How about a quickie before you leave for work?" followed by a wink to let me know she was serious. More than tempted to take Marie up on her offer of spending that morning exactly where I wanted to be, I decided it would be best to tell her "no," blaming it on a car I needed to deliver that morning, hoping it would upset her enough to start hating me, so when I finally said goodbye to this side of the living, it would be easier for her to move on to better things like the man I didn't recognize that made her smile more than I have over the past several years of my addiction.

With the cup of coffee designated for me still in hand, I excused myself from the garage and made my way inside the house I was now more than determined to save, to take what I was hoping would be my last shower before my permanent dirt nap, I barely managed to get my hair wet when I first heard the sound of a coffee mug shattering against the wall of the garage and Marie's feet stomping up the stairs to let me know this conversation was far from over. Once in the bathroom, Marie turned the water to its coldest setting so she had my undivided attention then pulled back the shower curtain, and with tears starting to form in those beautiful crystal-blue eyes with a hint of a future without me in them, asked if I even loved her anymore, followed by, "Please tell me what's really wrong?" reassuring me that no matter what it was, we would get through it together like we always have before—something that I knew would never happen if karma had anything to do with it. In an attempt to comfort Marie, I leaned out of the shower, kissed her softly on the forehead, before telling her that I loved her more than life itself and that nothing was wrong—something I don't think Marie believed since the conversation ended with the sound of her feet stomping back downstairs to the bar where I never make my special pan-sized pancakes anymore.

Once my last shower on this earth was over, I headed to the same room Marie and I have shared for the past twenty-some-odd years to get dressed for what I was hoping would be my last day at the dealership. After I got dressed, I decided that the insurance policy would be safer in the box of treasured moments Marie always kept in the top of our closet, instead of my back pocket along with a note of my last words to her that read,

Dear Pickles,

If you are reading this, it probably means I'm on the other side of life, please don't cry. I have caused you more tears than you deserve. I'm sorry for all the pain I've caused you with my addiction and hope one day—that you can forgive me even though I don't deserve it.

Enclosed you will find an insurance policy I didn't know I had that I found in a box. I'm fairly sure you already know about that is worth more than enough to stop the upcoming sale of the house we bought together so many years ago after answering that ad that seemed to be written just for us.

I will never be too far away from my one perfect everything; all you have to do is remember these three things.

When the wind blows, that's me kissing you, the same way I did for the first time at the falls. When the sun shines, that's just me reminding you of how perfect you are, and finally, when the rain falls, that's just me asking for more of that forgiveness. I'll understand if you don't give it to me.

Kiss the boys for me and remind them how proud I am for what they have become and that I love them no matter what your sister Sharon or her friend Merinda may tell them.

Signed,
Love Me

With my last words to Marie written down, I placed the note, along with the insurance policy in the box of treasured moments before heading downstairs, where she was sitting quietly to herself at the bar where I found the letter from the bank that she didn't know I had read and the keys to the old car that replaced the fancier one I had bought for her that the bank had repossessed due to lack of on-time payments beside her. Staring out the window with tears in her eyes while reminding me of the promise I made to never to lie to her again, and when I got home, we needed to talk about a few things that were more important than any customer or sale, a conversation I was hoping never to have. I cautiously grabbed the keys off the bar and made my way out the door like I had done a million times before leaving our relationship status to be determined.

Chapter 11

At Your Earliest Convenience

SOME PEOPLE SAY that love causes us to do the crazy things we do; as for me, I think its karma that's behind all the craziness, and love, is merely the tool she uses to get you to play the wicked game designed for her amusement only. A game that even though you have a 0 percent chance of winning, you are left with no other choice but to continue to play.

With the seven-figure insurance policy I was going to use to save the house Marie loved so much and the piece of paper with my final goodbye to her written on it both safely in the box of treasured moments I was usually absent from, I stood for a minute or so staring at the opposite side of the faded brown door from, where I left Marie sitting at the bar, or peninsula as Patty, the lady that sold us the house liked to call it, crying and no doubt questioning her decision to marry me twenty-some-odd years ago, before making my way down the stone walkway, past the big bay window to the driveway where the car that took longer to get going in the morning than me was waiting, careful not to look back at the house just in case Marie was watching me leave for what I was hoping would be the last time.

Once behind the steering wheel of the car I wasn't sure would start, I adjusted the rearview mirror, hoping to catch a glimpse of the people who were behind the laughing I wasn't sure I was hearing then adjusted the seat that was set for Marie, turned the ignition key, and patiently waited for the giant cloud of white smoke that let you know the classic clunker started to slowly disappear.

While waiting for the cloud of smoke to clear enough for me to see the end of the driveway, I grabbed some of the napkins from the front seat of the car and began wiping off the inside of the windshield when I noticed Marie standing in the big bay window beside the box I should have hidden before she obviously found it, crying the same tears that started when she interrupted my shower and drawing a heart on the fog-covered glass like she has done every morning since we first moved into the old house as her way of saying that even though I lied to her about all the events from the day before, she still, for some reason I can't explain, loved me. And as I watched Marie walk away from the big bay window, leaving the box with my name and the word junk written on it as a reminder that our conversation was far from over, I made a small request to the someone I don't think I believed in anymore to please take away the hurt I've caused her during my addiction so she could enjoy her better life without me then backed out of the driveway and started the long drive to the last place I wanted to be—the dealership.

So many different thoughts were going through my head as I drove past the several stop signs that lead to always-red traffic light at the end of our street—thoughts like who, from the dealership, was at the Jones's house trying to sell Mrs. Jones the newly redesigned Ford Explorer that early in the morning, especially with Mr. Jones car nowhere to be seen, and why did karma involve Marie in the game I already changed the rules to while she was too busy planning her next accidental event. After all, the only thing Marie did was live up to the "for better, for worse, for richer, for poorer" part of the agreement we made in front of the judge the day we became husband and wife twenty-some-odd years ago. With the traffic light taking a lot longer to turn from red to green, I decided to stop at of the corner store for a hot cup of my favorite-convenient-store coffee and hopefully a pack of smokes since the pack my brother gave me as a birthday present was somewhere in the same garage where Marie threw the cup of coffee she offered me against the wall after I told her some sale was more important than those few minutes with her.

Unlike those big chain convenient stores, you see on every street corner that sells made-to-order sandwiches and has huge walk-in coolers filled with every type of beer you can think of. This store was family-owned with a limited selection of beer, and all their sandwiches were made to order more than a couple of days before. The only advantage I had for doing any shopping there was that it was now owned and operated by my good friend Benny, who was usually okay with letting me put a few things on credit since every dollar I had was being used as a deposit on an if-come-maybe sale to Mr. Jackson. I worked with Benny for several years at the dealership where he was the most underrated mechanic and the toughest sale I had ever made until he took early retirement to run the store full-time after his wife inherited it from her father just four years ago. At more than a couple of years older than me with quite a bit more hair, Benny was a very soft-spoken, straight-to-the-point kind of guy and the only person I ever trusted to work on Marie's car.

Not wanting to be noticed by anyone from the neighborhood, who may actually know what's been going on behind closed doors of the house that was scheduled to be sold at auction in just six days from then, if I didn't make it to the other side of life, I pulled in the farthest parking space in front of the store and watched to make sure it was Benny behind the counter that morning instead of his wife. Who was a little less forgiving about our tab being paid a couple of days or months past the agreed-upon due date.

After a few minutes of making sure the coast was clear and watching memories in the rearview mirror of me walking with the boys down to the end of our street to get some candy from the stores—pretty impressive candy selection. I decided to go inside since my body was beginning to throw a fit for some nicotine and coffee just like it still does every now and then for those once-prescribed pills.

With my head lowered, in an attempt not to make eye contact with the same people that seemed to appear out of nowhere at the gas station where I didn't get a single drop of gas, and in the parking lot of the restaurant where my older brother bought me breakfast, I quickly made my way inside the store where, luckily, it was Benny sitting behind the counter reading the morning paper instead of his wife and straight to my favorite, several-hours-old, convenient-store coffee located at the end of the aisle where Benny kept all the "I'm sorry, I forgot some special occasion" gifts I've bought more than my fair share of over the past twenty-some-odd years Marie and I have been married. Once there, I grabbed the largest foam cup from the three sizes available, and while keeping a watchful eye on the people who suddenly appeared out of nowhere in the store's parking lot, I began adding several of those little plastic containers of creamer before filling the foam cup to the rim with the darker-than-usual coffee like my dad always did to prevent any extra dirty dishes in the sink since the coffee would do all the stirring instead of a spoon. After a few sips of the coffee my body was demanding and several words of advice from the voices in my head of how I could end my personal nightmare called life, I headed to the front register where Benny was reading the morning paper when I first came in and right into karma's next unforeseen, well-planned event that would test my sincerity over not wanting any more tomorrows, letting Marie out of our twenty-some-odd year marriage under the "death do us part" rule.

Growing up, I was always being told by someone or another to "pay attention" or to "watch where you're going," something I wish I was doing that morning instead of discussing with the voices in my head the best way to convince Benny for two packs of smokes and the cup of coffee I had already taken a couple of sips from until I got my next paycheck. Then maybe I would have noticed that Benny was no longer reading the morning paper like when I first walked into the store but instead was standing with his hands in the air at the request of a strange man wearing a black hoodie with matching ski mask and holding a gun, demanding all the cash from the register. It wasn't until after I accidentally knocked something off the rack of "I'm sorry, I forgot some special occasion" gifts that the strange man quickly turned the gun in my direction and began demanding all the cash I didn't have and the gold wedding ring that no matter how much my body was requesting those little pills I wouldn't sell.

People would later call what I did next an act of courage, pure bravery on my part, which would be the furthest from the truth. After all, those are two things that required a lot more energy than I had after twenty-four-plus hours without sleep. No courage and bravery had nothing to do with it; instead, it was an opportunity to finally end the game karma made me an unwilling participant in, finally quieting the voices in my head that have been reminding me of everything I had done wrong during my addiction since the first night of my unconventional rehab. It wasn't until after the strange man wearing a ski mask began pressing the gun he was holding firmly against my only clean secondhand shirt that I decided to take advantage of the opportunity to end my life by telling him to go ahead and shoot, causing what little I could see of his facial expressions to turn from angry and frustrated to just plain confused. After a few more empty threats of ending the life I didn't want any more if I didn't give him the ring I refused to part with, the mystery man wearing a ski mask decided to just grab the few dollars from Benny who had the same confused look on his face and quickly left the store while shaking his head in disbelief over what he just witnessed.

Feeling disappointed that the strange man wearing a ski mask and holding a gun lost his nerve to end the life I didn't want anymore, I took a couple more sips of the coffee I hadn't paid for yet and finished making my way to the front counter where Benny was already calling the local police department to report what would later be referred to as a botched robbery of a local man who just wanted a cup of coffee. Once I was close enough to hear Benny give a full description of the coward toting a handgun, who just exited the store with less than twenty bucks in the pocket of the dark jeans he was wearing, I helped myself to a cigarette from an open pack sitting on the counter that once belonged to an old mechanic friend of Benny's who recently quit smoking after losing his wife to cancer the day before and waited for whoever was on duty at the local police department to arrive. I would smoke three more cigarettes from the pack that belonged to someone I didn't know and drink two more cups of coffee I hadn't paid for yet before anybody from the local police department responded to Benny's call about a stranger wearing a black hoodie, jeans, and of course, a ski mask who recently robbed the store for less than twenty bucks from the register then ran out the door, shaking his head in disbelief over my request to end any chances of me seeing tomorrow.

After arriving on the scene, where I was hoping to be a chalk outline rather than a so-called victim, the friendly officer, who I met just a few hours earlier at the tracks where I had a minor run-in with the unexpected 2:15 a.m. freight train, began questioning me over and over about what exactly happened that morning until another friendly officer interrupted the questioning to see if I could identify a strange someone who was picked up just a block or two away, wearing the same black hoodie, jeans and carrying a ski mask similar to the one Benny described when he called that was found tucked away in the same pocket as a small-caliber weapon that wasn't even loaded and the less-than-twenty-dollar bucks that they believed came from the register. I hesitantly agreed before following the friendly officer I just met for the first time to the front of the store where his fancy car with the lights on top was parked with someone I recognized from my pill-chasing days handcuffed in the back seat named John something or another, who was once a proud husband and father of two children before he followed the same kind of instructions printed on the same kind of brown bottle his doctor gave him when he hurt his back at work after falling several feet off a ladder, costing him everything.

Following the friendly officer's request for me to take my time in identifying someone I already knew was the guy who held Benny's store up just a few minutes or longer ago, I spent a few seconds looking in the same eyes that were behind the ski mask threatening the life I didn't want any more before calmly telling the friendly officer it wasn't the guy, followed by "Yes, I'm sure" before he could even ask the question, figuring that there is nothing the judicial system could do to John that would be worse than living the life of an addict doing things you never thought you would do, going to places you thought you'd never go, chasing down those once-prescribed pills just to keep from getting sick.

The friendly officer, whom I just recently met, must have known I was lying to him about my friend John not being the guy who recently threatened to take my life if I didn't give him the ring I refused to part with because he would ask if I was absolutely sure John wasn't the guy that fit the description Benny gave several more times before finally allowing me to leave the scene of karma's recent well-planned accident designed for only her amusement. Now free to go about the business of making my inevitable suicide look like an accident so Marie could cash in the life insurance policy and save the house she loved so much, I walked over to where the new family clunker had been parked since I first decided to stop and ask Benny if I could put a cup of my favorite convenient-store coffee and two packs of smokes on my way past due account, something he allowed while we were waiting for anyone from the local police department to show up then began heading to my second day back at the dealership but not before waving bye to the friendly officer who was frustrated over me lying about John not being the guy who caused all the morning excitement everyone would hear about on the local news at 6:00 and 11:00.

Chapter 12

The Sixth Man

THE SIXTH MAN is a phrase often used in basketball to describe the unsung heroes who spend most of the time riding a bench, patiently waiting to fill in for the starters, whose name is on the back of most of the jerseys that the team sells. Allowing them to show that even though they don't sell as many jerseys as those other guys, they are just as good, and as it turns out, I had met the sixth man before; I was just too busy with my demise to realize it.

With another missed opportunity to save the house where I left my and Marie's relationship to be determined and a fresh pack of cigarettes in the pocket of the only clean secondhand shirt I had left, courtesy of Benny for ending the standoff with someone I lied about knowing, I started to become excited about not living to see another one of those consistent sunrises my older brother said something about a little over several weeks ago, finally ending the voices in my head and the game karma would soon regret forcing me to play. Karma must have noticed my newfound enthusiasm about taking tomorrow off my list of things to do because while I was listening to the harmony created by the family clunker's leaky exhaust and a song playing on the radio I didn't know the title to, karma began playing memories of times I had long forgotten, creating a debate between me and the voices in my head over the irrational thoughts I was having about everything being perfect after my so-called accidental death.

On one hand, what is a house? Except for the outside structure of a home that has a number and street name, so the utility, credit card, and finance companies know where to send the bill for items you purchased with money you don't have. In an attempt to make up for your absence from some kind of special event because you were too busy working, trying to pay for it by a specific date that's printed clearly on top of the bill they just sent you.

On the other hand, why should Marie give up any more than she has because of my inability to say no to those little pills that my body continuously demanded? After all, isn't not being able to have any kind of relationship with our oldest son, not to mention the three grandsons she so desperately wanted to meet for the first time, punishment enough for something she had nothing to do with? Besides, the strange man in the driveway I didn't recognize seemed to make her smile the same way I once did and would probably be a perfect replacement for the old broken-down addict that was me.

Over the next several miles, I continued the debate with the voices I was sure no one else but me could hear until I finally arrived at the last place I wanted to be, just in time to be more than a couple of hours late. After pulling into the only parking spot available, that just so happened to be right next to the tow truck that had what little was left of the car Matt the well-known secret picked for me to use the night before on the back, I sat in the driver's seat of the old family clunker that replaced the fancier one the bank was probably preparing for auction, smoking one of the cigarettes from the pack Benny gave me while looking at all the damage the 2:15 a.m.

train caused after I parked it on the wrong tracks and rehearsing the story of not only what happened to the car that I was now financially responsible for but why I was so late, a story I was sure no one would believe.

Once the cigarette I was smoking began tasting like the filter it had burned down to. I stepped out of the car to use the driver's side window as a mirror for a quick once-over, making sure my only clean second-hand shirt was neatly tucked in the second-hand pants I had been wearing since the day before and that the secondhand tie I was wearing was of straight, before crossing the less-than-busy street that divided the new car lot from the used one and straight to the door Marie had dropped me off in front of the day before, happy with the outcome of the debate I just had with myself that no matter what, I had to end my life.

There is a lot to be said about the peace you feel once you come to terms with your inevitable suicide and even though it wasn't enough peace to ease the pain of my heart, breaking over possibly not being able to kiss the one who's the best part of everything I am one again, I knew deep down inside that Marie was strong enough to endure the life we were supposed to spend the rest of together without me. And that the best thing I could do for her at that moment in time was end the life I was growing tired of.

With the appropriate finger used to acknowledge the couple of "Hey, part-time" chants coming from the salesman that was sitting on the benches just outside the front part of the showroom smoking cigarettes, I opened the door that I had been staring at for a second or two and headed straight for my new closet-sized office located directly behind where Matt sat all day, attempting to do my old job so I could postpone my boss's lengthy interrogation about my previous day's events long enough for me to rehearse the not entirely true story I planned to tell him, a couple more times in the privacy of my head.

Barely two steps inside the door I heard a slightly familiar voice with an accent that let you know they had eaten a spam sandwich or two, saying, "When a salesman shows up late the day after a sale, it probably means the customer paid too much." Trying to put a face with the familiar voice, I looked around to see who was behind the very distinct southern draw when I noticed sitting in the waiting area, watching the weather channel and enjoying one of that day fresh doughnuts, was Mr. Jackson wearing grease-covered overalls that had a red shop towel hanging from the pocket, a beat-up truckers hat with the logo of some oil company on the front, and an old dusty doctor's type bag at his feet.

Surprised to see Mr. Jackson there several days before Friday, I quickly greeted him with my usual "How are you doing, young man?" while extending my hand out for him to shake. After slowly standing up from the chair he looked more than comfortable sitting in, Mr. Jackson brushed all the crumbs that fell on the front of his overalls from the doughnut he was eating, wiped his hands off on the red shop rag hanging from his pocket before shaking my extended one, and replied, "I haven't been a young man for a very long time," while grinning a grin I had seen somewhere before.

I quickly reminded Mr. Jackson that he was just a little early by a day or two and that the 650 HP Mustang I put the deposit on the night before wasn't ready, but if he would follow me to the closet-sized office I was trying to make it to before I heard his somewhat familiar voice, I would be more than happy to get some of the lot guys started on it while we finished the paperwork part of his purchase. With one foot tapping the old dusty doctor's type bag he had brought with him that morning, Mr. Jackson said that it wouldn't be necessary for me to get anyone else involved just yet, and he just wanted to put some money down on the 650 HP Mustang like he didn't the night before. His only other request was the car be ready at 6:00 p.m. sharp that day instead of Friday so he could sign whatever paperwork needed his signature because he and his wife of forty-some-odd years were planning to be out of town for the next couple of weeks or so traveling to places I didn't bother asking where. After I agreed to his 6:00 p.m. sharp terms, Mr. Jackson grabbed the dusty bag he had been tapping with his toes, along with a couple more of that day-fresh doughnuts he seemed to enjoy, and began following me to my office where I left his paperwork just before the events that left me more than comfortable in my decision to end my life before Mr. and Mrs. Whatever Bought the House Marie and I raised our two sons in at the upcoming bank auction.

Once we made it through the maze that leads to my new closet-size office, Mr. Jackson took a seat in the only customer chair available while I sat in the chair behind my new old rickety desk, grabbed his paperwork, and asked how much of a deposit he wanted to leave. Chuckling as if I told a joke instead of asking a question, Mr. Jackson placed the couple of doughnuts he brought back with him on the rickety desk, then opened the old dusty doctor type bag that was resting on his lap, revealing several stacks of one-hundred-dollar bills, and said, "All of it, of course."

A little more than surprised to see what looked like more than enough to cover the five-figure amount we agreed on the night before, I began counting out the amount needed to complete the purchase from the several stacks of one-hundred-dollar bills while Mr. Jackson sat mumbling to himself, "A deal's a deal. A promise is a promise." Once I finished counting out the amount written on the buyer's order beside where it said balance owed, I excused myself and took the serval stacks of hundred-dollar bills, along with the purchase agreement Mr. Jackson signed the night before to the cashier for a receipt.

Convinced that the if-come-maybe sale to Mr. Jackson was part of karma's next wait-for-it moment she seemed to enjoy so much, I stood cautiously, watching over my shoulder while the cashier verified that I had counted out the right amount needed to complete the purchase then quickly returned to my office where Mr. Jackson was still mumbling to someone I had never seen, "A deal's a deal. A promise is a promise," with his receipt and the same ten-dollar-bill I used as a deposit on the 650 HP Mustang the night before as change.

After Mr. Jackson verified that the amount on the receipt matched the amount written on the buyer's order just above his signature, he stood up, brushed off the several new crumbs that had fallen on the front of his overalls from the doughnuts he seemed to like, then with the same smirk I had seen somewhere before, said, "I'll take the receipt. You keep the change. Consider it a day late birthday present so you can get something good for lunch or some gas for the old clunker you drove here" as if he knew about the never-ending game karma made me an unwilling participant in, without me saying a word.

Figuring Mr. Jackson was right about me probably needing some gas like I did after dropping Lennie off at his bachelor pad located in his parents' basement the night before, I accepted the all-too-familiar ten-dollar bill, placed it in the pocket of my only clean secondhand shirt, then walked with Mr. Jackson out to his black-and-brown nineties-something truck made by the same company that built the car he had just bought that coincidentally was parked on the opposite side of the tow truck that was carrying the car that karma demolished with the unexpected 2:15 a.m. cargo train seconds after I yelled several of those choice words and idle threats she didn't like very much.

Still convinced karma was setting me up for another well-planned, accidental event, I thanked Mr. Jackson for his recent purchase of the newer version Mustang he picked his wife up in for their first date and the ten-dollar bill that once belonged to my youngest son then watched as he drove down the less-than-busy street that divided the two different car lots yelling out his open passenger-side window in that familiar accent that let me know he had eaten a spam sandwich or two, "See you at six sharp. Make her pretty!"

With Mr. Jackson's old truck out of sight, I lit a cigarette from the "on the house" pack of smokes Benny gave me after what would become known as the "botched robbery of a local man who just wanted some coffee" and began slowly walking across the rarely traveled street to the showroom door Marie dropped me off in front of the day before, careful not to watch for any cars that may be traveling a little faster than the posted speed limit, in hopes of running into someone that was paying as little of attention to their surroundings as me, finally ending the frustration and misery that was occurring with every thought I had.

Now safely across the street I was hoping to get run over on, I wasn't at all surprised to see my boss impatiently waiting to greet me by the door I was trying to go in with a stack of papers I was sure had something to do with me being late that morning and, of course, the car he let me borrow the night before that was now valued at the current scrap price. He asked if I was done with the only customer I had since my return, Mr. Jackson, then directed me to follow him to the break room, where our meeting would take place out of sight to any potential sales that were being negotiated in the showroom at that time, just in case our meeting didn't go as smoothly as one might hope.

I followed him through the showroom, like a prisoner would follow a priest to the execution chamber, past the prying eyes of all the salespeople who were more curious about what was going on with me than their next sale, and down a couple of stairs into the break room, where the well-known secret Matt was sitting waiting for the stack of papers my boss was carrying that had the words disciplinary write up along with my name written across the top that would completely change the outcome of the game between karma and me that I was unwillingly invited to play just over three years ago.

Chapter 13

No Signature Required

WE HAVE ALL heard the unbelievable story about a single piece of the straw breaking a camel's back—a metaphor sometimes used to describe a unique event in our life that causes us to cut all ties with rational thinking. The same thing that happened to me when I realized I would have to explain all the events that occurred leading up to that moment to Matt, who was just a "well-known secret" about certain indiscretions that took place between my boss and the then aftermarket girl, Cindy something or another, nine months before he came into this world, causing me to question if my boss actually understood the definition of loyalty or was his just fictional like Santa Claus, the Easter Bunny, and the tooth fairy.

With the papers my boss was carrying now in front of him, Matt asked me to take a seat in one of the plastic cafeteria-style chairs across from him, so he could read line by line, section by section, of what I already knew those papers that had one of those yellow stickers that said "Sign here" meant. Deciding it would be best for everyone in the room, I stood out of arms reach of the well-known secret Matt and listened while he began reading from the stack of papers with the words "Disciplinary Write-Up Form," along with my name written across the top, like he was reading from a movie script, making sure to include the smashed car I parked in front of the wrong train at just the right time and my tardiness due to the unforeseen holdup at Benny's store by someone I knew who was holding an unloaded gun as the reasons for the actions they were taking against me. Once he finished reading from the script my boss gave him, Matt handed me a pen that I was sure once belonged to me and, with the same smirk on his face I've hit people over, told me to sign right next to the yellow "Sign here" sticker.

Ignoring the voices in my head that were telling me to put that pen in the area of Matt's body he was sitting on, I decided to choose my battles wisely and simply sign my alias, "Peter Pan," right next to where the well-known secret was pointing then slowly walked past my boss, who was monitoring our one-sided conversation from the doorway of the break room, making sure to give him the same look of disappointment Marie gave me when she realized that I had spent everything we had on those once-prescribed pills.

My dad once said, when talking about my biggest critic, I see every time I pass by a mirror or reflective surface, "You never want to mess with a crazy person" and that he honestly didn't know if the critic was crazy or not. A question I answered the first moment I saw Matt sitting in the break room with a pen I knew once belonged to me, and those papers with my name on top, keeping the answer between me and some old friends that have been keeping me company in the privacy of my head since as far back as I can remember. There must have been something different about me or I had a spot on my only other secondhand shirt that I didn't know about, because as I made my way to my office located directly behind where the well-known secret spent all day doing my old job. Everyone from salespeople to the cute couple who was trying to decide between the red, blue, or black car seemed to look at me a little differently than anyone has ever looked at me before. Almost as if karma had blurted out the answer to my dad's question about my worst critic as a warning to anyone that may cross in front of my path.

With more than a couple of hours between that moment and me delivering my if-come-maybe sale to Mr. Jackson that was now paid in full, I figured it was best for the well-known secret Matt that I keep myself busy, making sure Mr. Jackson's car was filled with gas and cleaned to the best of the lot kid's ability, only stopping long enough to eat what I was hoping would be my last meal that consisted of fried chicken and not my mom's self-proclaimed potato salad, hold the plastic spoon, fork, and napkin combos just like Marie and I ate on our first date at the falls, keeping it under the last ten dollars I had for the second time given to me as a late birthday present from my six o'clock sharp delivery.

Now as hard as it may be for you to believe, but at one time long before dinner, conversations only consisted of every-one who was attending looking at their cell phones, and a good day had nothing to do with the number of Facebook likes you received on a funny post that no one understands, from people you have never actually spoken to in person, purchasing a car was kind of a big deal. The whole family would get dressed in the latest and greatest "Sunday best" for a night out on the town to show off their recent purchase to anyone that may be at the restaurant they were going to for one of those long-for-gotten family dinners that are only spoken about during those "Do you remember when" conversations between old friends. And that's precisely the way Mr. Jackson showed up for his six o'clock sharp delivery time, except for the latest and greatest fashion part—unless you consider something right out of the late seventies, the current fashion trend.

Dressed in what can only be described as something right out of a 1970's Sears and Roebuck catalog, Mr. Jackson showed up right on time for his 6:00 p.m. sharp delivery, wearing a bright-green polyester leisure suit, complete with a butter-fly-collared shirt that didn't match anything else, and carrying the same old dusty doctor-type bag that was filled with cash earlier that day close to him. I greeted him in the same "How are you doing, young man?" greeting I used earlier that day then directed him to follow me outside to where the several years newer version of the same car he and his wife went on their first date in that just so happened to be parked in the same spot on delivery row where Helen parked her SUV the day the game between karma and me began.

Once outside, I light a cigarette from the on-the-house pack Benny gave me earlier that day, stood back, and watched as Mr. Jackson began inspecting every inch of the 650 horse-power GT500 Mustang in the always-popular "grabber blue," trimmed in the legendary white Shelby stripes while mumbling to someone I still hadn't put a face to "A deal's a deal. A promise is a promise."

After Mr. Jackson finished inspecting his recent purchase of a car I would soon find out meant more to him than I could have ever imagined, he began drying the tears that were starting to form in his "I've seen a lot of things in my life" eyes while I showed him how all the fancy options, he didn't seem to care about, worked. Until the well-known secret Matt paged me to my old office, where he was on the phone making dinner reser-vations for him and an "unknown someone" named Kim so Mr. Jackson could sign the last pieces of paperwork required when purchasing any car, truck, or SUV. With the dinner reservations for two made, Matt hung up the phone with the restaurant that had a fancy name then extended his hand out for Mr. Jackson to shake and said, "You must be Joseph?" Looking at me as if he was wondering who Matt thought he was, Mr. Jackson quickly responded, "Yes, sir, but you can call me Mr. Jackson," then took a seat in one of the customer chairs, completely ignoring Matt's extended hand. Now properly introduced, I excused myself so the two could get started signing the last few forms needed to complete Mr. Jackson's purchase and headed to my closet-size office I now occupied to plan my next unforeseen accident that would hopefully end my life and this silly game karma should have never invited me to play.

I barely got comfortable in the old chair behind my new rickety desk when I heard my name and "You have a call on line 3" over the loudspeaker that I just knew was Marie calling to finish the conversation that left our relationship to be determined earlier that day. Figuring this would be my last chance to tell her how much she was my everything before I made that seven-figure life insurance policy cashable, I took several deep breaths like I did before I kissed her for the first time down by the falls then pressed the button next to the little red flashing light on the phone in my new office and answered, "This is… How can I help you?" only to hear Marie's voice that sounded like she had been crying, saying, "Please don't say anything just listen. I need to tell you something important." In fear of her words being the reason I changed my mind of doing the right thing and dying, I told Marie that whatever it was, it would have to wait until I finished my delivery and that I would call her back after I was done—something I didn't plan on doing in hopes that she would be so angry at me that my recent demise wouldn't hurt her as much as the past three years I spent chasing those once-prescribed pills had and that she would spend the rest of her consistent sunrises with the guy that seemed to make her smile like I'm not sure I ever did then slowly hung up the phone while trying to ignore her pleas for just a few more minutes to tell me something I already knew about.

After slowly hanging up on the worst last conversation I was hoping to have with Marie before my upcoming recent demise, I heard Mr. Jackson, who was now standing in the doorway of my new office, holding the old dusty doctor's type bag tightly in one hand and an envelope with his copies of the paperwork he just signed in the other, clearing his throat as a way of letting me know he was there before making himself right at home in the small customer chair on the other side of the old rickety desk I was sitting behind so he could tell me the story behind him buying a newer version of the same car he and his wife took on their first date more than a couple of years ago.

Now clutching the old dusty doctor's type bag that was filled with cash earlier that day, a little tighter than before, Mr. Jackson spent the next couple of minutes asking someone who I still hadn't seen or been properly introduced to, "Where do I begin?" while looking around the small office as if the answer to his question was written somewhere on the old dirty walls. He then took few deep breaths and began telling me how, at one time, he was a top mechanic for some race car driver named Dale something or another, who drove the number 88 Quality Care car that allowed him to not only provide what he called a quite well-to-do life for his wife and two sons, but it also allowed him to travel from coast to coast, seeing things most people only talk about in one of those "I wish" stories we sometimes get lost in telling.

He continued the story by telling me about all the different cities he had been to, famous people he had met, and fancy parties he had attended more than once of all in the name of being what all husbands and fathers want to be when they grow up and that's a great provider to everyone that means everything to them—their family while keeping the most valuable asset they have to themselves—their time, until one day, you're left to live out the however many days you have left on this earth with the memories you never made and regret.

Mr. Jackson then spent a few extra minutes drying the tears he could no longer hide that were now falling from his "I've seen everything" eyes before finishing the story with a promise he made to his wife in which, one day, after he finally retired, they would spend the rest of their remaining years traveling to all the places he had been to without her. A promise he was determined to keep even though his wife had recently lost a long-fought battle with cancer just the day before and exactly forty years to the day since they said their first "I dos" in a small ceremony of just five people that included Mr. Jackson and his wife, who was now in an urn inside the old dusty doctor-type bag he had kept so close to him everywhere he went, which would now ride shotgun in the newer version of the old blue Mustang that he picked his wife up in for their first date just seconds before he fell in love with her for the first time—after all, "a deal's a deal; a promise is a promise."

After finishing the story I wasn't sure I understood, Mr. Jackson stood up from the broken-down customer chair he was sitting in, placed his hand on my shoulder like my dad would do as a way of letting me know everything was going to be okay, and said, "You see, life's not at all complicated. It's the people living it that make it that way, simply because we get so caught up in what the people in the marketing department of any major corporation says the perfect life is supposed to look like that we completely overlook what a perfect life actually is, and that's the memories we make, not the clothes we wore making them."

Now seeing a glimmer of the one thing in my life karma had no control over—hope—I placed my hand on Mr. Jackson's shoulder as a way of letting him know I understood what he was talking about then walked with him through the showroom, where the well-known secret Matt was impatiently waiting for me to finish delivering my if-come-maybe sale so he could make it to his dinner reservation with the "unknown someone" on time and out the showroom door where Mr. Jackson's new 650 HP Mustang that he referred to as simply "Pretty" was parked in the same spot, where karma made me an unwilling participant in a game I was sure I had just won.

Once Mr. Jackson was comfortable in the driver's seat of his new car and the old dusty doctor's type bag now riding shotgun in the passenger seat, I thanked him one last time for doing more than just purchasing a new car from me that he responded with "Don't thank me. Go home and thank the young lady who was on the other end of that phone call I couldn't help but overhear…," followed by "By the way, you can call me Joe. All my friends do."

With just enough hope to cancel any plans of ending those consistent sunrises my brother told me about the day I decided to get sober and Mr. Jackson well on his way to the first stop of the trip he promised to take with his wife, I finished smoking one of the last cigarettes I had left and headed inside where the well-known secret Matt decided to test the validity of my sobriety by saying, "Just imagine all the pills you could buy with this commission" that I responded to with a clutched fist across the nose of the well-known secret, breaking it before quitting the job that consumed so much of my time then headed home, to my soon to be previous resident, where I was hoping the most important someone in my life, Marie would be waiting.

Chapter 14

Dear Diary

FEAR IS OFTEN defined as an unpleasant emotion caused by the belief that someone or something is dangerous, likely to cause pain and or anxiety. As for me, I agree with my dad who told me after I watched one of those scary movies I wasn't supposed to watch, that fear is nothing more than the unknown, which would explain why I was scared to death during the short drive to my soon-to-be former residence, where I was hoping Marie had just enough understanding and forgiveness left for this slightly used addict who was determined to get his life back.

Now recently in between jobs and probably facing assault charges after breaking the nose of the well-known secret for questioning my sobriety, I began rehearsing with the voices in my head, that I had become used to, the truth, the whole truth, and nothing but the truth about the unbelievable events that started precisely forty years after I came into this world. Including the reason why there was a box hidden in plain sight that had my name with word junk written in big letters on the side that I was sure Marie had already found.

As I traveled the same route Marie had scribbled down after answering an ad that seemed to be written just for us about a house she immediately fell in love with, the first time we saw

Patty, our new realtor, standing on the front porch holding the keys that would unlock the freshly painted brown door of the house I was willing to give my life to save, karma began playing the few good memories I was present for like an all-day marathon of the greatest movies ever made. Memories like how the light from the streetlamp I was standing under the moment I fell in love with Marie made her crystal-blue eyes with just a hint of trouble behind them sparkle brighter than all the stars that were in the sky that night or how I hid in the bathroom of the hospital after the birth of each of our sons so no one would see me cry tears of joy while thanking the someone I was somewhat beginning to believe in again for such a precious gift.

Once I turned onto the street Marie and I raised our two sons on, I decided to drive around the block a couple of times to make sure that the unknown somebody, who seemed to make Marie smile like she hadn't since the start of my addiction, wasn't parked in the driveway like they were earlier that day after my brother picked me up from my first failed attempt to end my life with the always-on-time 2:00 a.m. train until the low fuel light on the new family clunker began glowing as if someone was telling me, "It's now or never."

With no other option but to finish the short ride to the house where Marie drew a heart on the big bay window earlier that day, I drove past a couple more houses that belonged to neighbors I don't think I had ever met then slowly turned into the driveway as quietly as the squealing sound the car made when you turned the wheel would let me so I could maybe smoke a couple more of those on-the-house cigarettes Benny gave me after my second failed attempt to clear my calendar of any more tomorrows before telling Marie the unbelievable truth about everything that had happened after she dropped me off at the dealership the day before.

It wasn't until after I put the family clunker in park and turned off the ignition that I noticed the house that would soon-to-be sold to the nice couple in the back at the upcoming bank auction was now as dark as it was the night before when I almost ran over Lennie who was trying to flag me down for our annual birthday smoke session, leading me to believe that the little bit of forgiveness I was hoping Marie had left for this lifelong recovering addict that used to be the man she fell in love with twenty-some-odd years ago was gone.

In preparation to have my heart broken like the day I came home only to find a small green backpack with everything I had left neatly packed in it and the note of so few words that meant so much Marie left for me shortly before I called my older brother for some much-needed help in my recovery, I sat quietly, chain-smoking one of the few cigarettes I had left from when I lied to the friendly officer about the someone I knew as not the guy who held the unloaded gun to my face because I knew they were still in the struggling phase of their addiction, listening to the sound of crickets chirping off in the distance and Mr. Jones's standing in his front lawn asking himself "where could she be at this hour."

With each drag I took from the freshly lit cigarette, karma began playing the other half of the memories that seemed to have gotten lost in my day-to-day struggle to be what all husbands and fathers want to be when they grow up and that's a great provider to everyone that means everything to them—their family. Memories like how the boys would stand with plate and fork in hand, waiting for some of my special daddy's home pancakes I haven't made in I don't know how long or how beautiful Marie looked fast asleep on the couch wearing the red dress she bought for our twentieth-anniversary dinner after dosing off, waiting several hours for me to arrive home late again.

Deciding to take the "It's now-or-never approach," I took a couple more drags off the last of three cigarettes I had left before putting it out in the foam cup with just enough of my favorite gas station coffee left in it from earlier that day to make it the perfect ashtray then began the long walk down the stone walkway, past the big bay window where I could see several banker's type boxes, including the one I was now positive Marie had found, scattered about as to say she was fully prepared to move on without me and to the front door that was long overdue for some fresh paint, hoping with each step I made that my key would still fit the lock like it did the night before.

Now as nervous as I was the first time I told Marie that I loved her, I slowly turned my key that seemed to still work the lock and slowly opened the door, only to find Marie sleeping on the secondhand couch, wearing my strawberry-jelly-stained secondhand shirt from earlier that day surrounded by the boxes I noticed from the big bay window that was filled with notebooks dated from that day all the way back to when I first met Marie the summer before my senior year of high school.

Careful not to wake Marie, I made my way around the several scattered notebooks and boxes that I noticed from the big bay window on my way to the front door so I could cover her up with the same blanket we used on our first date at the falls that she must have borrowed from my parents' house with no intention of ever returning it then began reading every memory I had somehow forgotten about that was clearly written in Marie's handwriting.

Dear Diary,

I just let my friend, Shelia's boyfriend, borrow my car, so he could deliver some of his what he calls his freshly cut green stuff to one of his friends, but I knew what they were talking about hint, hint, and if my parents found out they would kill me but I'm so glad I did because I met someone well sort of I was so tongue-tied diary after seeing him standing on a loading dock of some kind of machine shop in an area I didn't know existed wearing a Batman shirt acting as nervous as I was when I said yes to going out with him next Friday and even though he gave me his number I forgot to ask him his name wish me luck.

Dear Diary,

Oh, diary what a fantastic night our first date was. He took me to the most beautiful place it was right next to some waterfalls where we laid out a blanket and ate from a picnic basket he packed with cold fried chicken and potato salad that was a little bland for my taste then spent the rest of the night looking up at the stars which you know diary has always been my dream date.

Dear Diary,

Sorry, it's been so long since I have written you, I've been spending every waking moment with hopefully my future husband, don't be mad diary but I have to tell you something I'm pregnant!! I know, I know we are young, and he hasn't even graduated high school yet, but I don't care if I spend the rest of my life living on the sleeper sofa in my parents living room all I want is him this baby, and whatever else life hands us as long as he is there with me.

I looked through more of those boxes so I could read every moment of our life together that I spent all these years overlooking while chasing a fool's errand for a place whose only concern now is placing an ad to find my new replacement for the second time.

Dear Diary,

Happy twentieth anniversary to me and another missed date night that at one time was a mandatory once a week thing even if it was just snuggling up in front of the fireplace in the living room of this miserable house that I now spend countless hours walking around in thinking of him. Now it's just another empty place setting and me in in the sexiest red dress I could find ready to rock his world but instead, Mr. and Mrs. Richardson needs a new van so of course, he's going to be late again. Just like all the other times, he missed birthday parties, baseball games, and graduation for that stupid dealership. I would rather live in that box that Mr. Jones sat out at the curb tonight from the latest and greatest refrigerator that I'm sure he'll want to buy because he's always trying to keep up with him. Maybe I should just hook up with a random someone, and perhaps that will get his attention, but more than likely, he'll just try to sell them a car or warranty besides diary, I love him too much.

Dear Diary,

Forgive me I had to draw a line in the sand today, I packed all his stuff up neatly in a small green backpack and left it outside with a note that said so few words but meant so much. He looked so sad diary, standing outside in the rain looking like a lost puppy. I hope his older brother is right and that he will call him to finally end his addiction to those once-prescribed pills. I'm not at all upset over everything that's at the pawnshop or that he sold on those Facebook buy sell trade groups. Those are replaceable, but he isn't, help me find the strength diary.

With tears now starting to form in my "seeing things for the first time" eyes, I read through a couple more of those notebooks I had never seen before, including the one that led up to the real events that began shortly after the guy on the radio lied to me about what a beautiful day it was going to be that Marie was now holding close to her chest.

Dear Diary,

It's been twenty-eight days since I sent him out to find the man I fell in love with the summer before his senior year of high school and his sobriety diary. I was hoping the kiss on his cheek, and me telling him that I still think he was sexy after twenty-some-odd years of marriage would make his day better, but sadly diary I don't think he believes me. Not that he thought I was lying, but I'm pretty sure it's just the disappointment in himself.

Dear Diary,

I hope his day is going good. I'm sure everyone there will be asking him all kinds of questions that he won't want to answer about where he's been all this time and all the weight he lost recovering from those miserable pills; hopefully, he'll just quit that miserable place.

Dear Diary,

Me and our youngest son got our tips from the sandwich place today, so we went in together and got him a birthday cake, along with some decorations; after all, it is his fortieth. Now they aren't the fanciest, just some different-colored letters that spell out Happy Birthday that I can hang on the mantel of the large stone fireplace so they are the first thing he sees when he comes home. Shoot, diary, I dropped his cake and smashed it a bit—oops, I must be getting tired. I think I'll take a nap, TTYL.

Dear Diary,

I had the strangest dream last night after I fell asleep waiting for him to come home from his first day back at that miserable dealership. It started with me looking out the bedroom window I like to keep open during these brisk fall nights when, all a sudden, I heard his voice scream out, "I love you, pickles," followed by the whistle of the always-on-time 2:00 a.m. train. Oh, diary, I hope he's okay. He didn't come home last night after dropping Lennie off at his bachelor pad in his parents' basement, and I just found a banker's type box in the garage, where anyone could find it, that had his name with the word "junk" written on the side, filled with all the pictures I've framed for him over the years. As if that's not enough, diary, I'm almost positive he found the letter about the upcoming sale of this miserable house I can't stand spending all the time alone in. I'll call his brother. I know he will help me find him, WML.

Dear Diary,

Good news, diary, his brother found him. He didn't tell me where or why he was out all night, only that he would bring him home after they got a bite to eat. Diary, the day just keeps getting better. While I was waiting for him to come home, our new landlord came by to drop the keys to that cute little duplex I looked at the other day as a backup plan to this miserable house that he seems to care about so much. Now maybe he will quit that stupid job, at that stupid place, and just get a job at Benny's store—I mean, after all the milk, bread, beer, and cigarette at state minimum prices we have bought there, not to mention how long they have known each other, I'm positive Benny would hire him, and with the money I make at the sandwich place, we could do it, diary, I know we can. In fact, diary, I'm so sure that we can do it. I'm going to tell him to just quit that place the first chance I get. I promise, diary, I promise.

After reading all of Marie's private thoughts that were written in her handwriting, I finally knew what a fool looked like; after all, I was wearing his shoes. I had just spent the past twenty-some-odd years trying to give Marie everything she didn't want while keeping the only thing she did want to myself—my time.

In an attempt to keep the tears that were now falling down my face to myself, I placed the notebook Marie was clutching so tightly against her chest on the floor beside the couch where she was sleeping and headed to the back patio or "watchtower" as Marie liked to call it for a little privacy, only to find my youngest son quietly sitting and eating something leftover from the night before.

Still trying to hide my tears from anyone else that may or may not have been watching me, I sat down in one of the old busted-up patio chairs located on the opposite side of the deck from where my youngest son was sitting, lit one of the last cigarettes I had left, and began talking with the voices in my head that, for some reason, hadn't gone away about what my next move should be in this game called life that karma had been playing so eloquently.

Several minutes passed of both me and my youngest son quietly looking out at the backyard where the old swing set and sandbox were when, out of the blue, my youngest son said, "I see you read the notebooks Mom's been writing in every day for I don't know how long." A little more than surprised that he knew about the books written in Marie's handwriting long before me, I simply responded, "Yep." Then while nodding, my youngest son said something I had heard once before, "So you now know that Mom doesn't need you, right?" He must have been able to tell by my facial expression that his statement would require a little bit of explanation because he quickly followed it with, "The fact that Mom doesn't need you leaves only one conclusion of why she is lying there on that beat-up couch, reading all the good times you overlooked in your quest of something none of us understood, and that's she wants you. Not the latest and greatest anything thing you can buy her, but for you, the person she fell in love with the moment she met you the summer before your senior year of high school." He then stood up from the other busted-up patio chair he was sitting in, reached in his pocket, and handed me another ten-dollar bill so I could buy some more cigarettes that I had recently run out of before walking back inside the house he grew up in, leaving me speechless.

Now shocked by my son's "She doesn't need you" speech, I decided to take a walk down to Benny's store for another pack of smokes and to complete a job application that would lead me directly in the path of karma's perfectly timed plans to end the game I refused to participate in anymore, testing everything I had learned during my short recovery from those once-prescribed pills.

Chapter 15

Like All Good Things

"EVERY CLOUD HAS a silver lining" is a phrase often used to put a positive spin on every difficult or sad situation we experience in life as a way of making us feel hopeful even though things didn't go quite like we planned, which would explain why I was still walking in a vertical position instead of Marie cashing in the seven-figure policy to save a house she didn't seem to want.

Still, a little more than shocked after reading about all the things I had been overlooking for the past twenty-some-odd years, chasing a fool's errand for the perfect life described by the people in the marketing department of any major corporation to sell you the latest and greatest whatever they are selling, I placed the recently acquired ten-dollar bill my youngest son gave after he explained the "She doesn't need you" speech, my older brother mentioned something about the first day of my recovery in the pocket of my last secondhand shirt, along with a pen to fill out my first job application in forever and headed down the street to Benny's place for some cigarettes, a job, and maybe a cup of my favorite gas station coffee, deciding to walk instead of drive since I didn't want to find out how far the new "family clunker" would go after the low fuel light came on.

A lot of things have changed in the soon-to-be old neighborhood since Marie and I first answered the ad that seemed to be written for us so many years ago yesterday. And with every step, I took towards what I was hoping to be my new place of employment to replace all the chain-smoked cigarettes I had that day. Every memory that I never made was replaced with several what if I had done this? questions we sometimes ask ourselves after a big something or another happens to us, in order to whisk our fragile minds away from our now reality.

Questions like what if had broken the unwritten rule in retail that states "When a customer is that mad, never make eye contact?". Would I have ever known how miserable Marie was spending all those alone times in that miserable old house? Or what if I hadn't sold everything, we owned feeding addiction to those once prescribe pills? Would I have known that Marie simply loved me for who I am, not what I could give her, making me one of the few people that has actually kissed the most beautiful girl in the world. With each drag I took off my last cigarette, I asked myself several more of those "what-if" questions until I noticed some smoke and what looked like fire coming from of all places Mr. Jones's garage.

Convinced this was karma checking to see if I had been paying attention in her class—"Life 101"—I took a few deep breaths and began walking down Mr. Jones's driveway that was outlined with several freshly trimmed shrubs and a large stone wall to the garage where I noticed the bright lights I saw from the street wasn't fire, but instead, the taillights of a silver Mercedes with license plates that read, "Her Baby," wanting to quickly finish the pop quiz I was sure karma was giving me right then. I opened the garage door to let out some of the steam-like smoke that had been flowing from the exhaust of the fancy gift Mr. Jones bought for his wife the day I came home from my unconventional rehab at my brother's house, only to find it was Mr. Jones sitting in the driver's with his head resting on the leather-wrapped steering wheel with tears falling from his closed eyes.

Not sure if Mr. Jones's suicide attempt was a success or not, I stood back, watching for signs of life before placing him in the upright position so I could reach around the leather-wrapped steering wheel he was resting his head on and turn off the ignition, hopefully preventing him from doing what I had failed miserably at twice since my fortieth birthday the day before.

The sound of the motor going silent must have woke Mr. Jones's up because as I was trying to put the key in my pocket out of his reach, Mr. Jones quickly grabbed my hand and began mumbling, "You don't understand." But little did he know, I completely understood the feeling you get when seeing tomorrow is not an option, and for the first time, you feel completely at ease with the decision to end your own life.

Using what little bit of energy I didn't have left since I hadn't slept in a little over forty-eight hours or so, I pulled Mr. Jones from the front seat of the fancy car his wife didn't seem to want anymore and out to the driveway for some much-needed fresh air. Once Mr. Jones finished coughing up whatever it was in his lungs like I do every morning when I first wake up, I asked him the standard "What could be so bad in your life?" question everyone seems to ask when they don't understand why a loved one would prefer to die than see another one of those consistent sunrises I never really appreciated.

After slowly standing up, Mr. Jones wiped the tears from his eyes that he had to have known I saw then reached into the inside pocket of his suit that probably cost more than mine and Marie's recently acquired family clunker and handed me a note that I could only assume was written by Mrs. Jones's that said so few words but meant so much:

I can't live like this anymore. I have found someone that loves being with me more than trying to keep up with the people down the street from us best of luck and goodbye.

—Kim

In disbelief that the note I had just read seemed to mirror the one I got from Marie not long ago when she sent me out to find the man she fell in love with and that Mr. Jones's first name was the same as mine, I decided it was time for me to use some of the lessons I had learned about life, love, addiction, along with some other stuff over the past couple of days, trying to cash in the insurance policy to save a house Marie cared nothing about, starting with those consistent sunrises my older brother told me about the day he saved my life.

Not sure where to start the awkward conversation between me and Mr. Jones since we had never been properly introduced to each other, I began looking around the driveway as if the answer was written somewhere on the ground before asking the same question my older brother asked me the first morning of my recovery.

"Do you know what makes sunrises awesome?"

In what I could tell was out of pure frustration, Mr. Jones rolled his eyes the same way my sons would after I told them one of my signature dad jokes and answered, "No, but I bet you're going to tell me."

Now wearing the same grin I had seen on my dad's and older brother's face more than once, I replied, "Consistency" then began repeating word for word, the same thing my older brother told me while drinking a cup of his high-octane coffee.

"You see, no matter what's going on in our own little worlds, good, bad, alive, or dead, that sun is going to come up, and the only thing that is just as consistent as the sunrise is shit happens! No matter if you're a good person, bad person, it's self-inflicted, or no fault of our own, shit will happen, and that the key to surviving those consistent sunrises is to simply make sure you know where your shoes are so you don't get any of the shit between your toes." After a quick chuckle, Mr. Jones placed his hand on my shoulder before inviting me into the house I had only seen the outside of in passing so he could grab a fresh pack of the same brand cigarettes I smoked and something cold for us to drink.

Still acting as a crutch for Mr. Jones, who was still chuckling over my brother's sunrise answer I had just told him, we slowly walked down a stone walkway that was outlined by perfectly trimmed hedges, passed a big bay window where I noticed a couch that matched the fancy one I sold in one of those Facebook buy sell trade groups sitting in the living room, to a huge front door that didn't need a single coat of paint.

Now able to stand on his own two feet, Mr. Jones slowly opened the door that led directly into what I assumed was the living room since the fancy couch I noticed from the big bay window was sitting in it. The room wasn't what you might call huge, but the size wasn't the main attraction to it; instead, it was a massive stone fireplace with pictures of every family vacation his wife and their two sons I didn't know he had taken without him neatly arranged on a solid oak mantle that would be the perfect place to hang Christmas stockings.

Still following Mr. Jones's lead, we made our way through the dining room, where I'm sure he missed more than his fair share of those "How was your day?" dinners with the family, then passed a bar, or "peninsula" as Patty, my and Marie's former realtor like to call it, and into a very modern average-sized kitchen, where Mr. Jones grabbed two packs of the same brand cigarettes I smoked from a carton sitting on top of a fancy refrigerator where he grabbed us the something cold to drink he mentioned something about, before heading outside to a well-maintained patio where I couldn't help but notice a swing set and sandbox that looked like it hadn't been used in sometime, sitting in the middle of Mr. Jones's freshly mowed lawn.

Now comfortably seated in one of the fancy patio chairs that were a lot more comfortable than the plastic ones Lennie and I used during our annual birthday smoke, I sat quietly, chain-smoking a much-wanted cigarette, listening to Mr. Jones hum the same song about the end of the line Lennie did his worst karaoke to during the ride home to his bachelor pad at his parents' house the night I decided it would be best for everyone I cared about that I end my life until Mr. Jones suddenly stopped humming, long enough to ask me the one question I wasn't sure I was ready to answer.

"So how are things on your side of the block?"

After calmly taking a drink of the whatever cold to drink we were dinking and lighting a second cigarette from the fresh pack Mr. Jones gave me, I took a deep breath, before saying something I never thought I would have to say, "Not at all like I had hoped life would be. You see, I'm an addict and proud survivor of the opiate epidemic that you hear about on the news that no one talks about until after the funeral of a loved one who lost the battle," followed by all the unbelievable real events that led up to me having this conversation with him now, including the always-on-time 2:15 a.m. train that left me on the wrong tracks for just in time for the right train, the holdup at Benny's store by someone I knew who I falsely accused of NOT being the one who pointed the unloaded gun at my face since I understood the hell he was going through, and how I just left the most beautiful girl in the world sleeping on our new secondhand couch in a house that would be sold at auction in just four days from then, surrounded by boxes of notebooks I had never seen before that had everything I overlooked in the past twenty-some-odd years of marriage written in Marie's handwriting.

After my open confession about everything in my life not being as perfect as I lead myself to believe, Mr. Jones took a quick drink of the cold whatever we were drinking and a long drag of the cigarette he was smoking before responding to everything I had just told him with just one word, "Wow!"

Over the next several hours or so, Mr. Jones and I sat outside, watching the moon replace the sun in the sky, talking about everything that had happened in our lives over the past twenty-some years we lived on the same street without even saying a simple "Hi" to each other. Things like how proud we are of our kids even though our relationships with them wasn't what you might call the best and how different it is being a grandfather at what we called our young age. We even talked about how foolish we were to believe that the guys in the marketing department of every major corporation actually knew what a perfect life was.

Now a couple of hours into the next day and confident we wouldn't have another car running in the garage situation, I finished my last cigarette, thanked Mr. Jones for his hospitality, and began walking down the driveway to the sidewalk so I could start the short walk to my soon-to-be previous resident where I left Marie sleeping on our new secondhand couch surrounded by several notebooks I had never seen until that night when, all of a sudden, it hit me—no, not something philosophical like I would begin pursuing a better tomorrow without letting what I had done in the past interfere with my next consistent sunrise because, like I said, in the beginning, my story is a lot simpler than that. No, what actually hit me was a 2013 Ford Explorer being driven by the well-known secret Matt that replaced me at the dealership after twenty years of dedication, who was so distracted by the oral conversation he was receiving from an unknown somebody he had just had dinner with that he didn't see me standing under the same streetlight I was now looking up at.

With everyone that was gathered around my so-called accident now inside their homes uploading the video they made of my unforeseen accident to Facebook and all the blood that was donated by yours truly now washed away by the rain that had been falling, I began listening to the sound of the sirens that were on the special van, the unfamiliar face who diagnosed me as being stable, put me into for my ride to the local hospital, where after only a short stay I was finally able to go home with a newfound confidence that no matter what I had done in the past, life would only get better for everyone I cared so much for.

I have to admit, I was a little surprised by everyone who gathered at the old house after I was released from the hospital. There was my older brother who taught me to always remember where my shoes were to get through those consistent sunrises. My youngest son, Austin, who never gave up on me and my recovery from those once-prescribed pills, Lennie, my best friend, who I knew always had my back, and of course, Mr. Jones, who was not only a lot like me, but as it turns out, he was one of the top personal injury attorneys in the area and would be handling my lawsuit against the dealership pro bono since it was his soon-to-be ex-wife, Kim, that was giving the well-known secret Matt the oral conversation that distracted him enough not to see me step out into the street, even my oldest son, Zachary, who I hadn't spoken to since karma made me an unwilling participant in the game I'm pretty sure was for her pleasure only, stopped by to see me with his three sons and new wife that he met shortly after he divorced his first wife, whose name I never cared to remember.

A lot of things have changed since the night of my so-called accident that I was sure karma had something to do with. The upcoming sale of the house to the nice couple in the back was canceled after Mr. Jones paid the amount we were past due to the bank as a way of thanking me for somehow saving his life. Lennie finally moved out of his bachelor pad located in his parent's basement and into the cute little duplex Marie wrote about in those notebooks I didn't know even existed until that night. My older brother still makes custom furniture in the workshop behind his house, where my youngest son, Austin, helps out from time to time to learn some of the things I wish I would have taught both my sons. The calendar that hangs beside the coffeepot where Marie and I have our morning meetings is now marked up with the dates my oldest son, Zachary, will be visiting with the grandsons, allowing Marie to be what she has wanted to be for some time now—a grandma. As for me, well, I live in the last picture we ever took together as a family, centered on the fireplace mantel in a fancy frame that reads, "Because someone is in heaven, heaven is always here" with the dates September 2, 1973, to September 4, 2013, precisely forty years and two days since I came into this world, twenty-seven days of my sobriety, and just one day short of learning to live again.

Most people would consider my death as another cruel act of karma, as for me, I think it was the most compassionate thing she had ever done because even though she knew Marie had already forgiven me for all the things I had done wrong chasing those once-prescribed pills, she knew I like everyone else struggling with addiction could never forgive myself.

The End

About the Author

C. S. BEAR is a proud survivor of the opiate epidemic we hear about every day on the local news at six and eleven.

He spent three years, two cars, a house, and several relationships with loved ones, chasing those once-prescribed pills in order to feed his addiction until what some may call his "unconventional rehab" in 2014.

After 6 plus years of sobriety his goal now is to maybe show, those who have never battled with addiction, the other side of the story that's usually ignored until right after the funeral of a loved one who lost the battle.